How To Format Your

Picture Book

for

Createspace & Kindle

Without the Frustration

A. Olson

How to Format Your Picture Book for Createspace &
Kindle Without the Frustration

Contents

How To Format Your
Picture Book
for
Createspace & Kindle
Without the Frustration

Introduction

You've written your book. Now you are ready to publish it. You have two choices for publishing a hard copy: Lulu or Createspace. They are the two most popular and well-known outlets. This book will cover formatting for Createspace, especially for children's pictures books.

Formatting a novel is straight forward. Though I will cover that in another book. Picture books for kids can be very frustrating to format properly. In the last few months Createspace has tightened the rules on proper formatting and are more stringent with their review process. As a result, what might have worked a year ago won't any more.

I have studied their guidelines for picture formatting and have written them here in an easy to reproduce manner. However, there are programs that you will need to invest in in order to create your images. I've listed them here:

Microsoft Word (Most computers already come with them installed if you pay for a product key upon purchase.)

Adobe InDesign (This can be purchased and downloaded from the Adobe website. However, it is pricy and you can spend up to $700 to get the full version. Though they have introduced their creative cloud which is a subscription service. You pay $9.99 per month for the full version of the software.) I highly recommend this software for the creation of image heavy books for print.

Bookcover Pro. (This software costs about $115 and works well for formatting basic book covers. But it's not as good as Photoshop. It only allows you to place images in the cover, but offers so filter effects or text special effects.)

Photoshop (This is another program from Adobe. It is one of the best and is considered industry standard, but you will pay a hefty sum for it. Though, again, you can get access to it through Adobe's creative cloud for $9.99 a month.)

Serif Draw Plus (This is another imaging software program, and is European in its origin, and has most of the features Photoshop has. It costs about $80.)

PaintNet (This is a free program and can be used to resize images. It is very basic in the features it offers.. It can be downloaded here: http://www.getpaint.net/)

Adobe Acrobat (This program is a must have for converting your files into pdf format for uploading to Createspace. It costs about $300 for the standard and that will serve your purpose.)

Gimp (This is a free image editing software which has many of the features Photoshop has. If you do not want to invest in Photoshop, Gimp is a good substitute and highly recommended.)

I've listed the programs above so that you can go through them and decide which you wish to purchase. You may even already have these on your computer. Buying these programs are an investment, but one worth making if you choose to format and publish your own books for years to come. As a self-publisher you will be using a variety of software to format your books properly.

Createspace Margin Guidelines

Page Count	Inside Margin	Outside Margin
24-150 Pages	0.375"	at least 0.25"
151-300 Pages	0.5"	at least 0.25"
301-500 Pages	0.625"	at least 0.25"
501-700 Page	0.75"	at least 0.25"
701-828 Pages	0.875"	at least 0.25"

Print Books with Full Bleed

A full bleed book is a book with images that fill the entire page, from edge to edge. This is the most popular way to format children's books.

Open your image editing software. I use Photoshop. I made the decision to ditch the free software and just purchase the CS6 version and have not regretted it. Click on *file—new project* and set up your image size, bleeds, and margins. For instance if you are creating an 8x10 book then you will need to create and 8.125" x 10.25" image. This is because Createspace requires that your images extend beyond the page margin: 0.125" for width and 0.25" for height. The formula goes like this:

Width trim size + 0.125 = total width

Height trim size + 0.25 = total height

So for an 8x10 book your images and interior pages must be formatted to 8.125 x 10.25 in dimension.

For a 5x7 book with full bleeds, pages in the interior file must be 5.125 x 7.25.

This is why I format images to the full page dimensions so that when I create the interior file, the images do not look blurry. And if you want to play it safe, make your images larger than the page size. For instance, if you are making an 8x10 book, you can make your images 9x11. Once your new project is created, you will have a blank canvas.

Formatting your Images

Open Photoshop (or Gimp if using it) and start a new document.

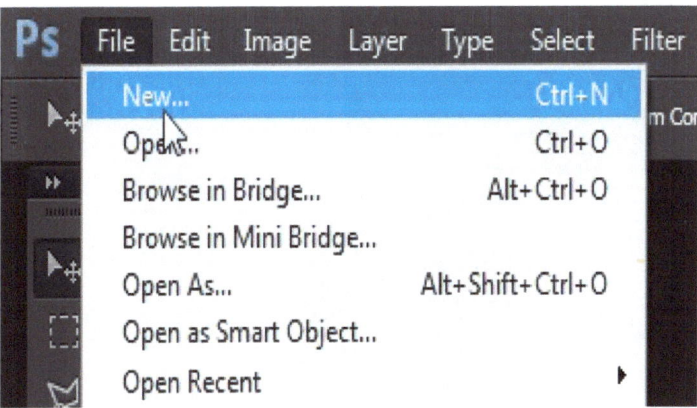

And you will get the New Document dialog box. Set the size of your document larger than you page size. For instance, if you are doing an 8x10 book, then make your images 9x11 with a resolution of 300 dpi.

Click *Okay* and you will get a blank canvass.

Add your image by selecting the

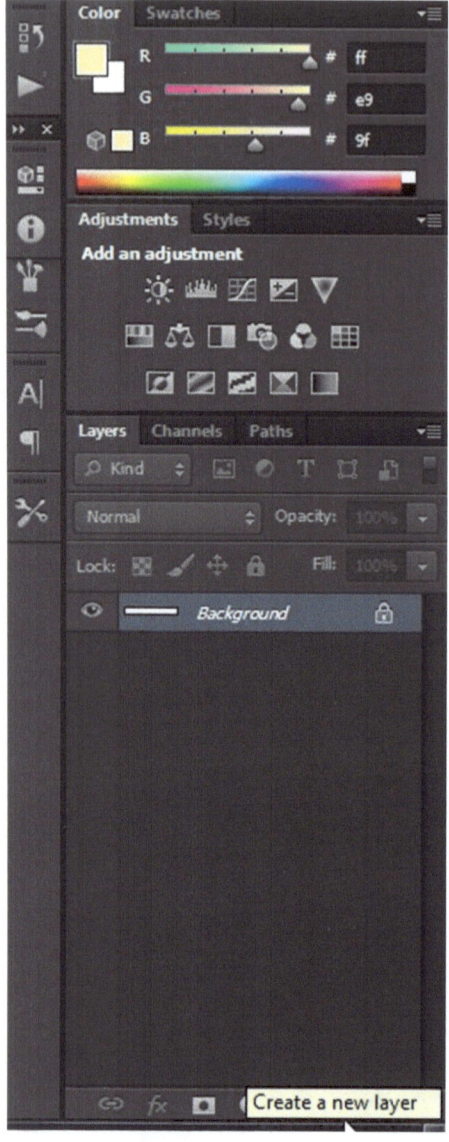

new layer tab in the bottom right corner.

Go to *File—Place* and select your image file.

Next, you need to put in your guides, marking your margins. Createspace requires that all text and live elements (anything that you don't want to get cut off in the printing process) be a minimum of 0.25 inches from the edge of the image. I recommend making that space 0.5 inches. This gives you more room away from the trim edge and will ensure that nothing gets cut off. And it keeps Createspace happy.

Note: If you are formatting your print book in word, it is best to have the text already embedded in the image. If you are making a kindle book only, you still need to have your text embedded in the image. If you are using InDesign for your print book, it is up to you whether you embed the text in the image, or choose to add it in InDesign.

Go to *View—New Guide*. First we'll will put in the vertical margins, so make sure that vertical option is selected. The first guide is easy. It will be set at 0.5.

Once it's in, you will need to go to *View—New Guide* again and put in your second vertical guide. Now, you need to do some calculations. Our images is 9x111. So that means that the second margin needs to be 9 - 0.5, making it 8.5.

Go back to your guides dialog box (*View—New Guide*). Make sure horizontal is selected and type in 0.5. Repeat the process, except your second guide will be set at 10.5 (11 – 0.5 = 10.5).

Now you should have a canvas that looks like this. Also, you can change the color of your guides by going to *Edit—Preferences—Grids & Guides* and select your preferred color.

Now it's time to put our image on our canvas. Go to *File—Place* and select your image. Photoshop will stick it in. Just stretch it until it covers the canvas.

Next insert your text. Make sure you use a font size and color that can be read against the background of your image. I recommend using a serif font such as Garamond or Minion. You want a font that is crisp and easy to read. You might want to also bold the font so that it stands out against your image.

Click on your text tool.

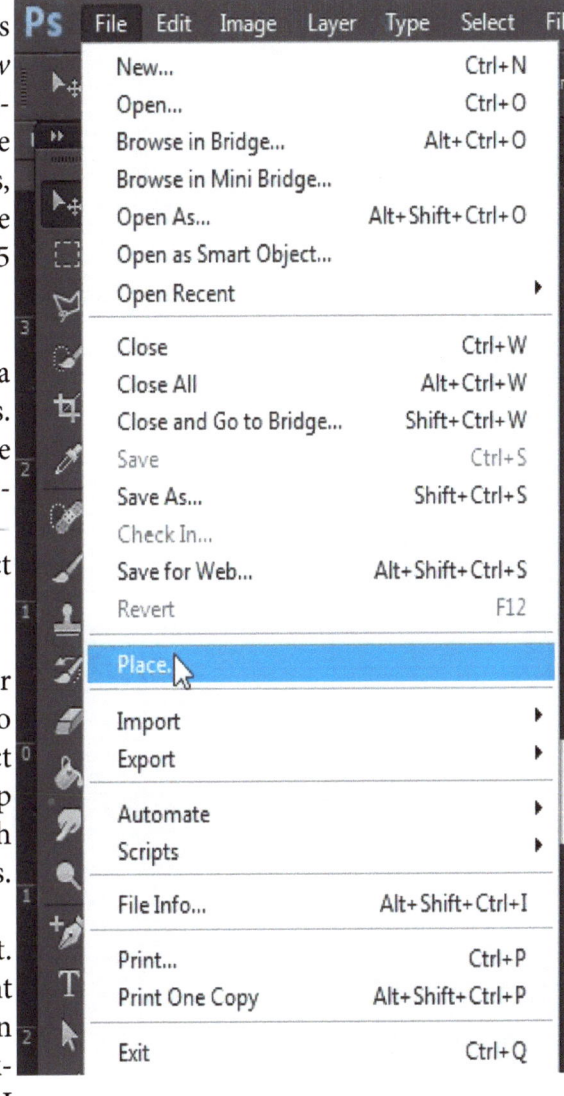

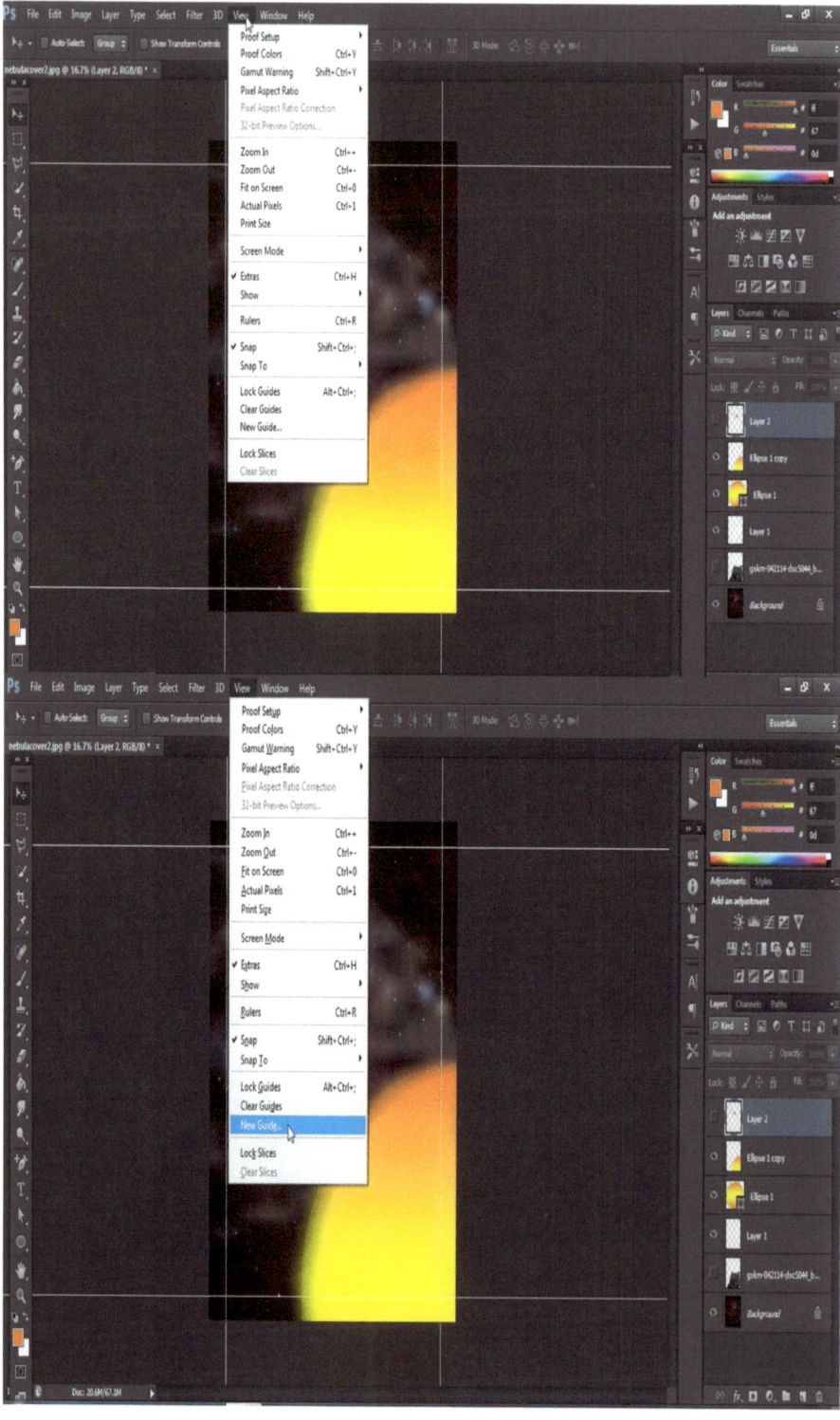

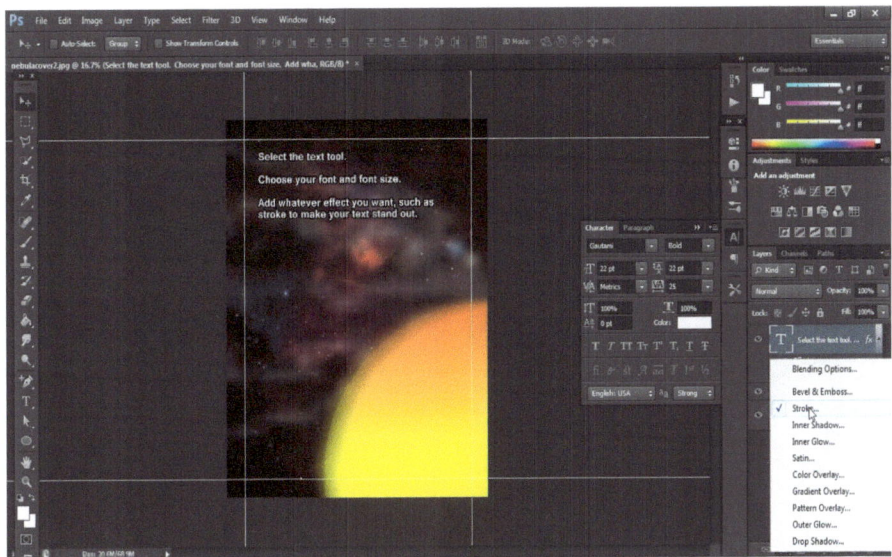

And just select an area within the margin lines you had put in where you wish to place your text.

Make certain that the text stays within the inside margins. If it extends beyond those lines, Createspace will reject your file.

Once you have finished formatting your image and inserting your text, double check that the spelling is correct. Then save your image as a jpeg at 300 dpi. Label your file in a way where you can easily locate it. I usual-

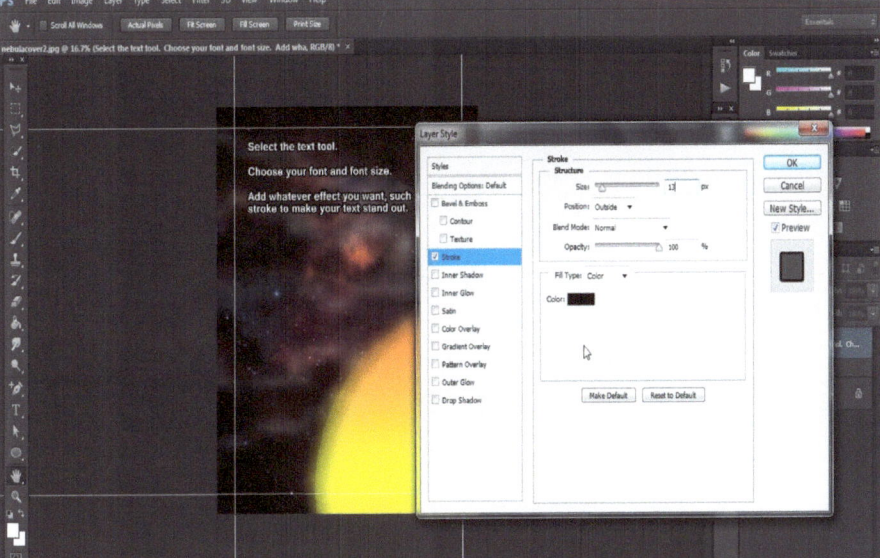

It is best if you put your page number on the image itself.

Make sure that the odd page number is on the bottom right hand side of your image. If it's an even page number, then put it on the bottom left hand side.

ly set up a separate folder on my desktop for my print books and label each image *page 1, page 2,* etc.

This is a time consuming process so be prepared to spend a few hours on this.

Once all of your images are created, it is time to create your interior file for Createspace. As I've said before, I prefer using InDesign for setting up my interior files for Createspace. It is easier to use, more reliable, and InDesign is a layout and publishing software, whereas Microsoft Word is a word processor best for typing. However, not everyone has InDesign and it is possible to create a kids book with full page images in Word. I will discuss both.

Full Bleeds Formatting in Microsoft Word

Open Microsoft Word and start a new project. Go to the margins setup and click on custom.

You will want to set up your margins according to Createspace's guidelines. I've reproduced them here.

Your book is probably no more than 32 pages. Either way, you will be using the margins for the 24-150 page range.

Go to your margins setup and select custom. Fill in the inside and outside margins according to the chart. Use a gutter margin of 0.375". Then, select *mirror margins*. After that click on the pages tab in the dialog box and select custom page size. For the height type in your trim size plus the 0.125. So if you are using an 8x10 book size, type in 8.125. For the height

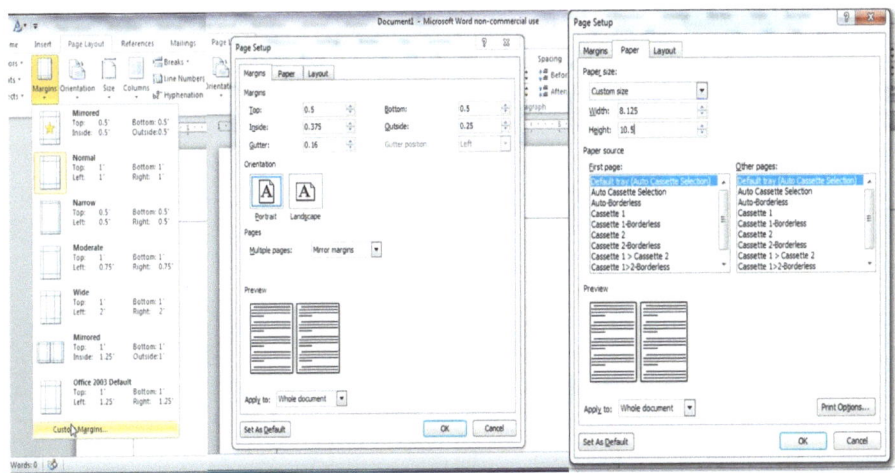

type in the height plus 0.25. (i.e. for an 8x10 book size the height would be 10.25) Click okay.

Now your document should be ready to go. Create three sections. Go to *Page Layout—Break—Section—Next Page.*

Set up your Title page, and copyright page in the first section. I usually just center everything. Your title page should just have the title of your book and your name.

On the copyright page I usually put something like this:

> This is a work of fiction. Names, characters, places, and incidents within are the product of the author's imagination or are used fictitiously, and any resemblance to actual persons, living or dead, business establishments, events, or location is entirely coincidental. The publisher does not have any control over and does not assume any responsibility for author or third-party websites or their content.
>
> Your book's title
>
> Copyright © year and name
>
> All rights reserved.
>
> No part of this book may be reproduced, scanned, or distributed in any printed or electronic form without permission. Please do not participate in or encourage piracy of copyrighted materials in violation of the author's rights. Purchase only authorized editions.
>
> ISBN-13: (Put your assigned ISBN number here.)
>
> ISBN-10: (Put your assigned ISBN number here.)
>
> Printed in the United States of America (*Only put this part in if you are printing in the United States.*)

Next put in your dedication page. At the end of the last word of your copyright page, hit enter. Then, go to *Page Layout—Break—Section—Odd Page*.

The dedication page usually consists of a single sentence about whom you want to dedicate the book to. Then press enter and insert another odd section break.

Once all of that is done, you are ready for your images. First, you want to go to *File—Options—Advanced*. scroll down to *Image Size Quality* and make sure that the *Do Not Compress* box is checked.

Also, you will want to go to *File—Options—Save* and make sure that the *Embed text* is checked and that the two boxes below it is unchecked.

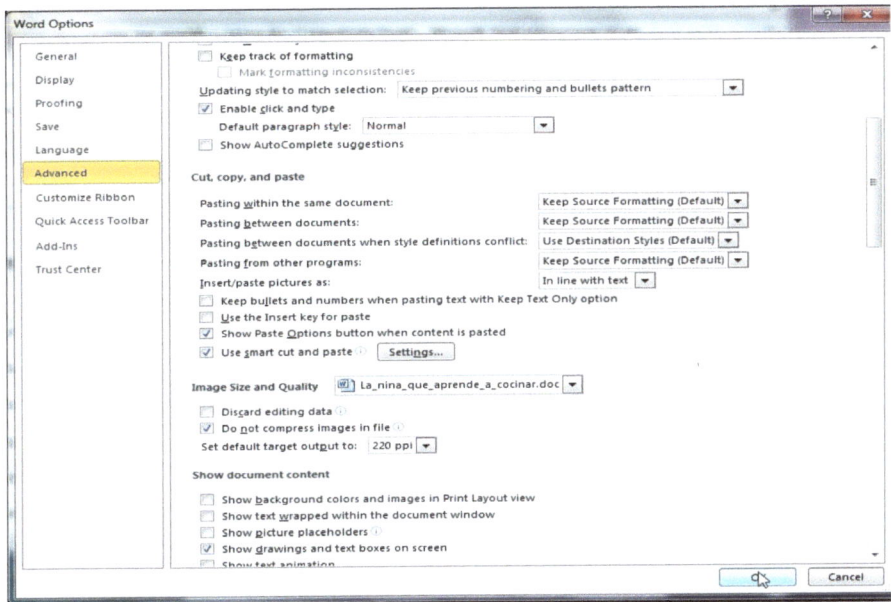

Now, go to the page where you will insert your first image and click on *Insert—image* and select the first picture. Click on your image. Go

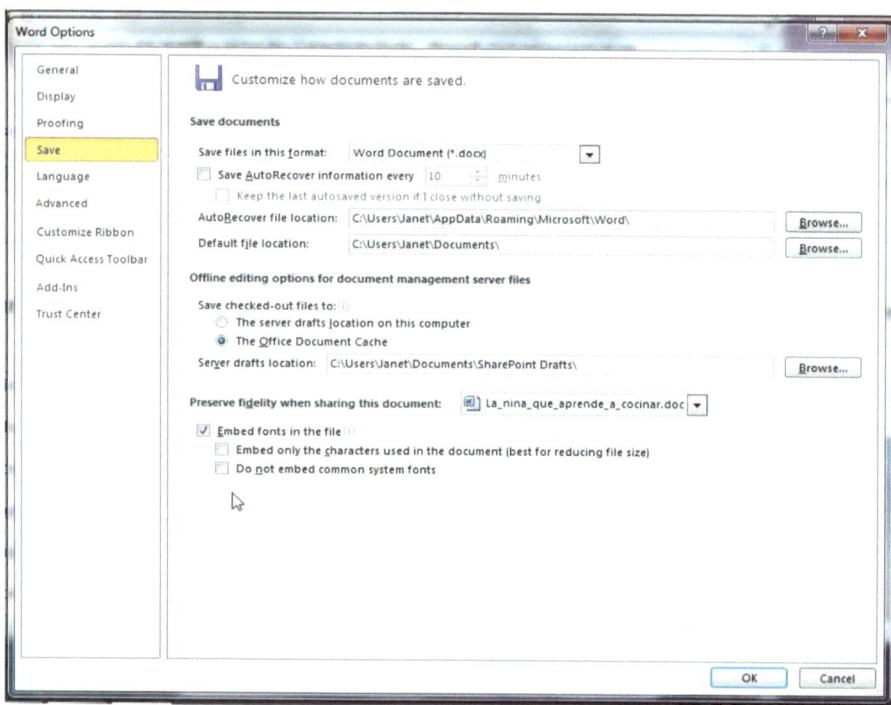

to *Wrapping—Behind Text.* Then open the image size dialog box. Make sure that the *Lock Ratio* and *Relative to Page* are unchecked. Then put in the height and width of our image so that it matches your page size. For an 8x10 book your image should be 8.125 x 10.25. However, because Word loves to shrink images, you might want to type in 8.16 for the width and 10.7 for the height. Drag the image if necessary to center it and so that it covers the page from edge to edge. You may have to zoom in to make sure that there is no white edge around your image. Repeat this for all of your images.

Hit *ctrl—enter* to insert a new page and repeat the process with inserting the next image, until all of your images have been placed in your document.

Save constantly!

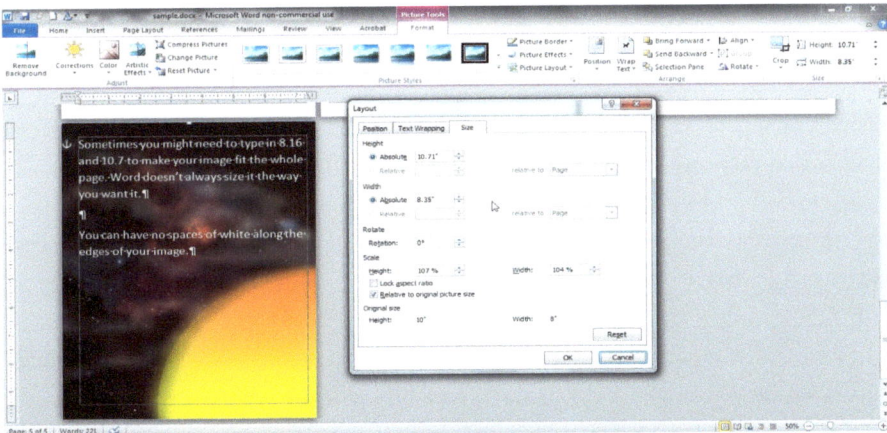

After every image is added click the save button in case Word freezes up, which it has a tendency to do when working with a lot of pictures.

Once you have finished inserting your images, go to section three of your document. This is where you add an *About the Author* section. Your personal biography written in the third person. It only has to be two paragraphs in length, but it lets your readers know a bit more about you. This section is also where you can list your other books that are already published or will be released soon.

Save one last time and close the file.

Open Adobe Acrobat. Click on Create New PDF. Select your book file. Microsoft Word will save your file as a pdf, but I never use it since it usually screws up the formatting. Using Adobe PDF to convert your file works best.

Once your file has been converted save it. Then, scroll through it and make sure it looks the way you want it to. If it doesn't, then go back into your word file and make the necessary changes. If it does save one last time and close the file. Make sure your pdf file is less than 40 MB. If it isn't you can save it as a Reduced Size PDF. Createspace won't accept files that are over 40 MB.

Yes, Word has a save as PDF function, as one reviewer has mentioned. but I have never found it to be reliable. Usually what happens is your fonts will be un-embedded and the images could shift. If you want to try it, go to *File—Save as PDF* and click okay.

However, I prefer using Adobe Acrobat to convert a word file to PDF. It is more reliable and consistent in what it turns out. Yes, Adobe costs money, but as I've said before, self-publishing is something you want to do on regular basis, you might want to consider investing in these software programs.

There are other options as well. You can always go to Fiverr and ay someone $5 to convert your document to PDF, or go to Zamzar (http://www.zamzar.com/convert/doc-to-docx/.).

Note: Sometimes even when you format your book properly, Createspace will still reject your interior file. This is usually due to some small issue that their system detects and has to be fixed on their end. Or it is something so minor that you will never find it and need them to tell you specifically what it is. If this happens to you, call Createspace directly and talk to their technicians.

For instance, I had a PDF file that kept getting rejected by their review system. My source file was set up properly. After calling Createspace and spending time on the phone with one of their technicians, I learned that the text on one of the images went just a millimeter over the gutter line which was enough to make them reject my file. To fix it, I just reformatted that image. It saved me hours of needless work.

Just fill out the form and they will call you in five minutes.

Full Bleeds Formatting in InDesign

Open your InDesign program. Click on *New Document* and set it up. Put in the margins and the number of pages your document will have when done.

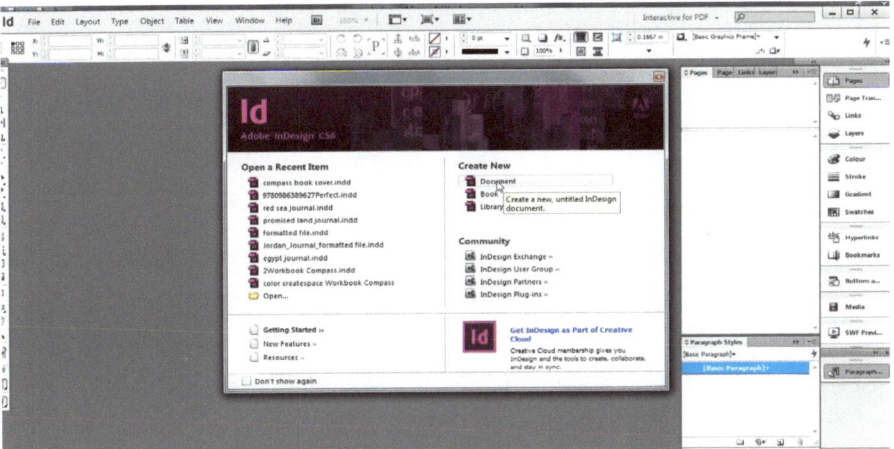

You'll go to the page sizes up and type in the width and height. Since we are using 8x10 as our example, that would make the page size 8.125x10.5. Make sure your margins are set at 0.5 inches. Set the gutter margin at 0.375.

The first page in the document will be the title page. The second page is the copyright page and the third will be your dedication. The fourth remains blank and the fifth page is where you start putting in your images.

Click the type tool and stretch the box across the first page.

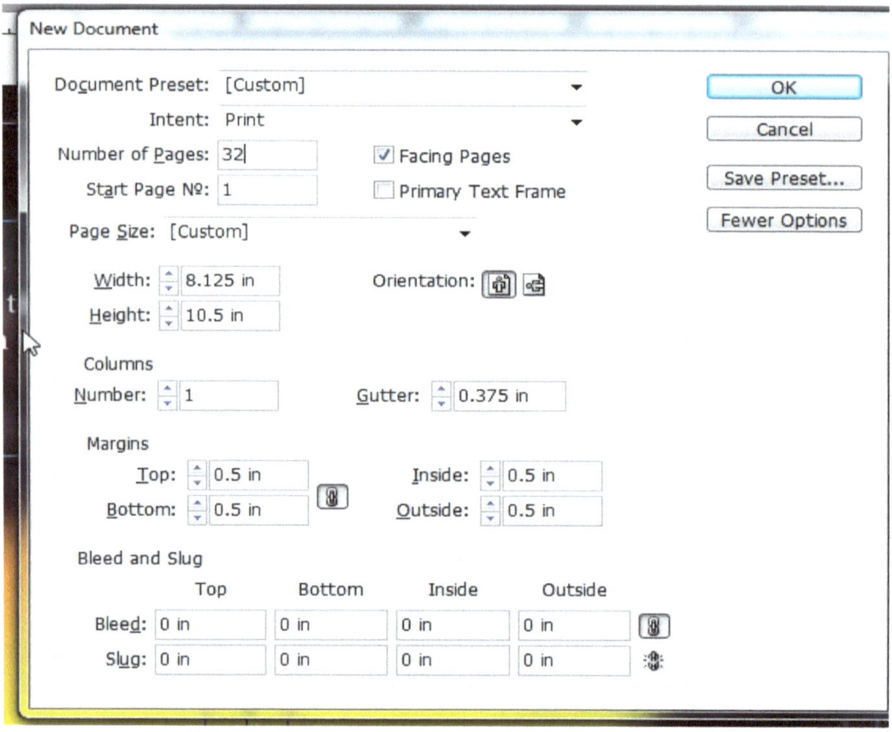

New Document

Document Preset: [Custom] ▼   OK

Intent: Print ▼   Cancel

Number of Pages: 32   ☑ Facing Pages   Save Preset...

Start Page №: 1   ☐ Primary Text Frame   Fewer Options

Page Size: [Custom] ▼

Width: 8.125 in   Orientation: 🔲 🔲

Height: 10.5 in

Columns

Number: 1   Gutter: 0.375 in

Margins

Top: 0.5 in   Inside: 0.5 in

Bottom: 0.5 in   Outside: 0.5 in

Bleed and Slug

	Top	Bottom	Inside	Outside
Bleed:	0 in	0 in	0 in	0 in
Slug:	0 in	0 in	0 in	0 in

Type Tool (

You can use the select tool to size the text box so that it edges touch the margin lines.

Type in the title and author name.

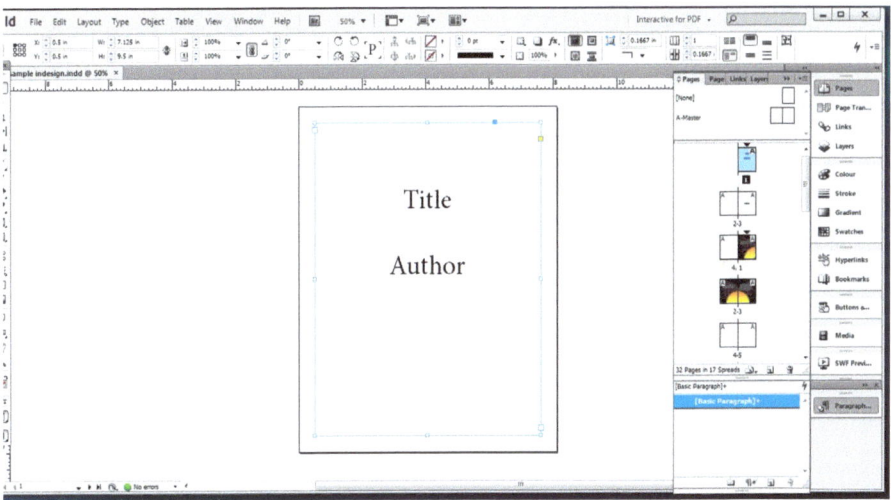

Repeat the process for the copyright and dedication page.

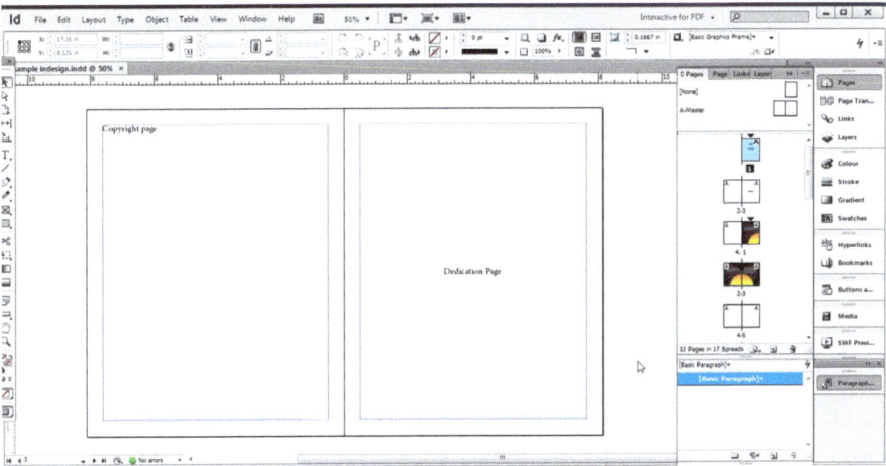

You can center text on the page very easily with InDesign. Use the select tool to select the text box with the text you want centered on the page. In this example, I used the dedication page. Click on *Object—Text Frame Options*.

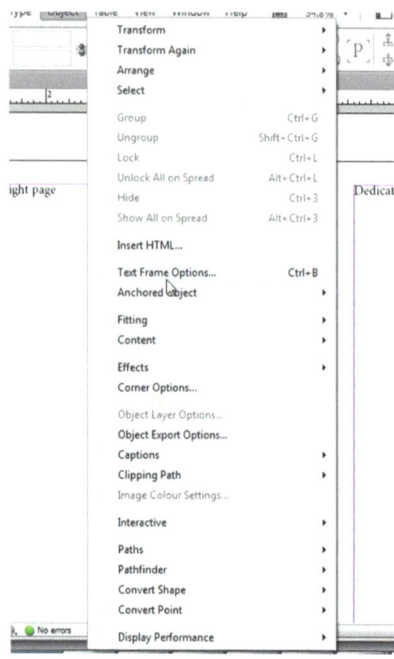

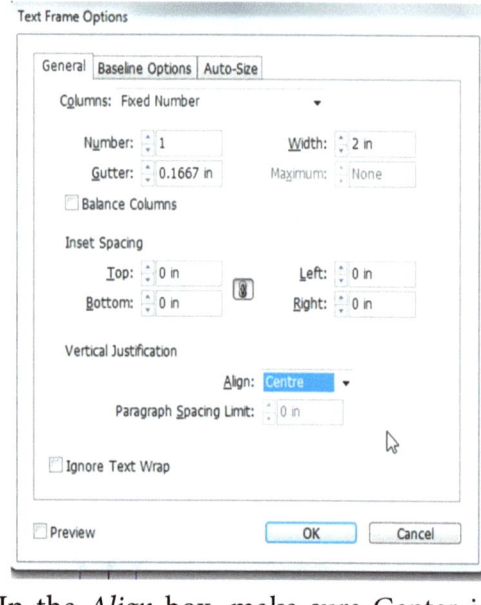

In the *Align* box, make sure Center is selected. It may be spelled Centre. In-Design tends to use British spellings, not American.

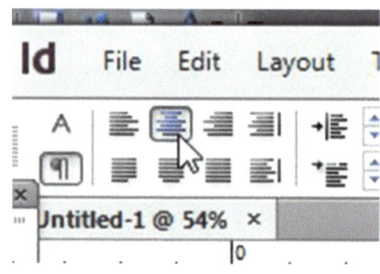

Then go to the paragraph area and hit the *Center* button.

The text will be perfectly centered.

Next, we need to insert the images. Click the rectangle tool and stretch a box across the entire page you want the image on. Because the page size is 8.125x10.5, then the rectangle box needs to be the same dimensions.

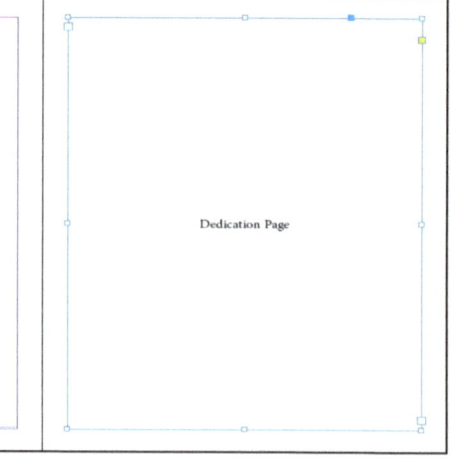

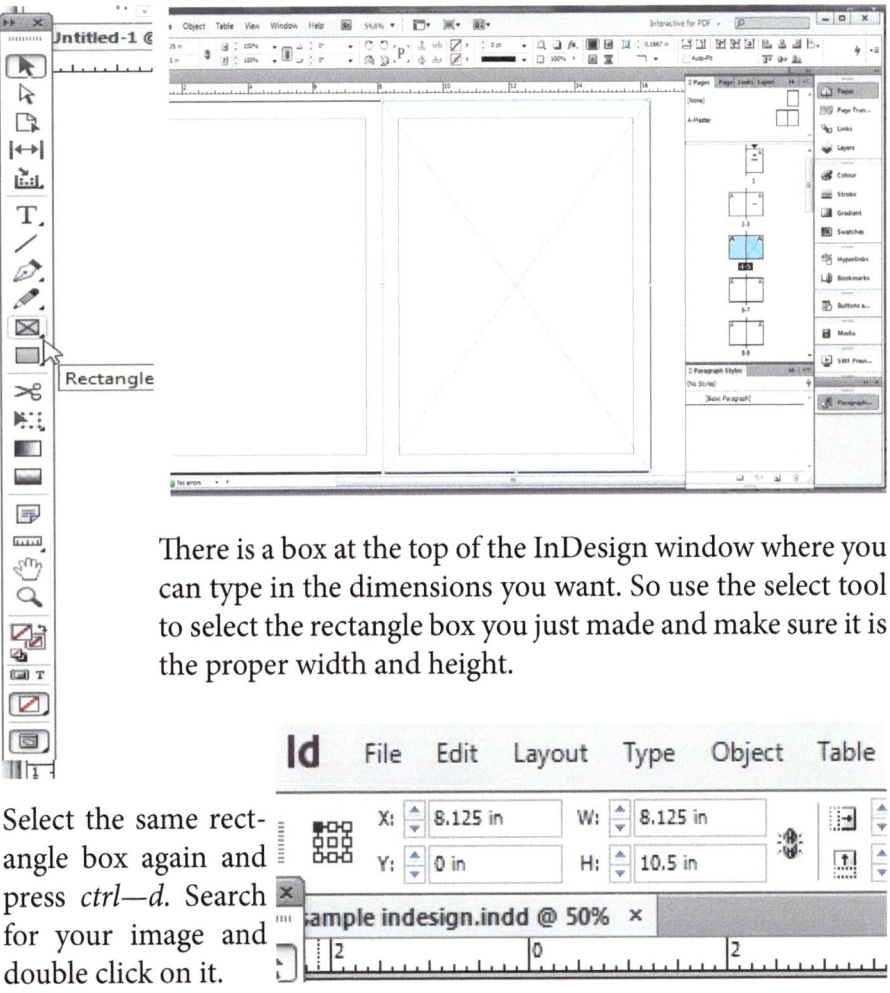

There is a box at the top of the InDesign window where you can type in the dimensions you want. So use the select tool to select the rectangle box you just made and make sure it is the proper width and height.

Select the same rectangle box again and press *ctrl—d*. Search for your image and double click on it.

Next, you need to make sure that the image fills the entire box you made, so right click on it, scroll down to *fitting* and click *fit content to frame*.

And the image will fill the frame and the entire page. Repeat the process until you have inserted all of your images.

When using InDesign to format your picture book, you don't have to have the text already embedded in your image. You can add the text directly to the file.

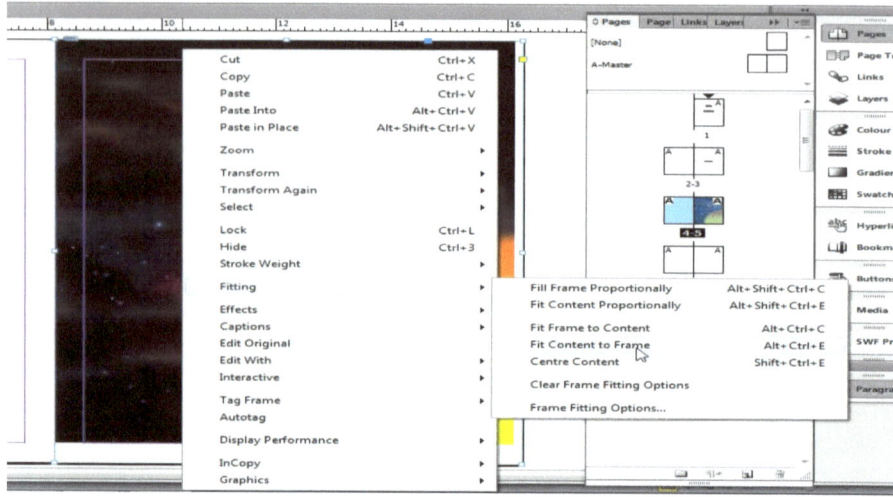

Note: If you already had the text embedded in your image then you can skip this part, as there is no need to add the text again.

To add text to your file, click on the text took and draw your text box, making certain that it is well within the margin lines.

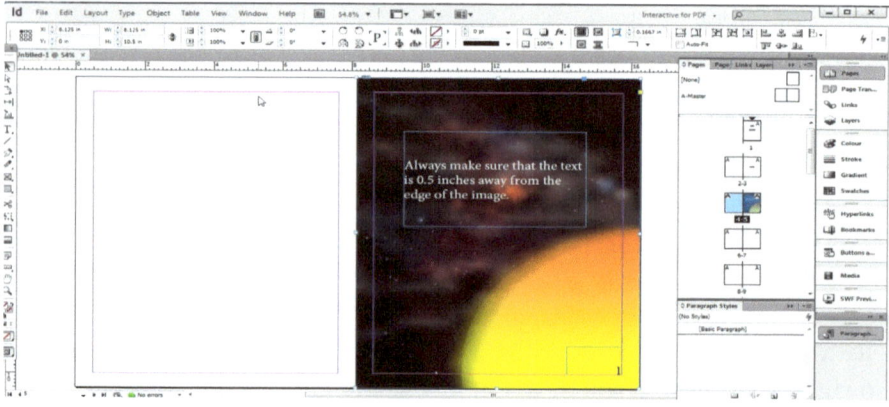

Format your text using the font and paragraph formatting tools. You can bold or italicize text. And just like in Word, you can center, left align, or right align your text. InDesign also has a left justify, center justify, and right justify function.

Choose your paragraph alignment.

Then choose your font (or character) and font size.

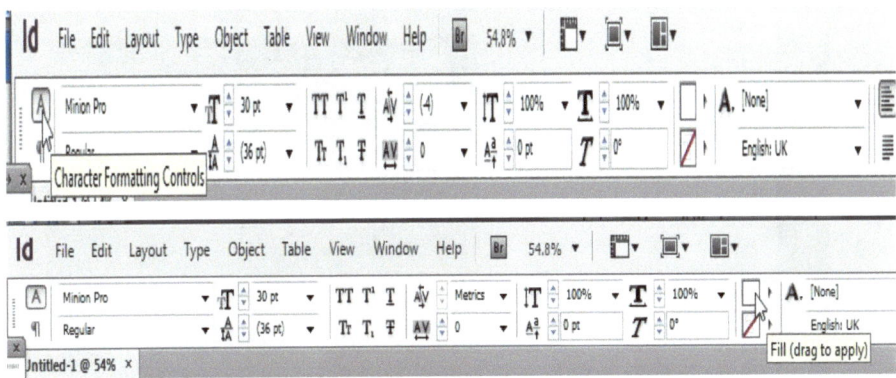

You can also choose the color your text and add a stroke outline if your wish.

Then decide if you want the text hyphenated or note.

Note: InDesign tends to automatically hyphenate text, so make sure the box is unchecked if you do not want your text hyphenated.

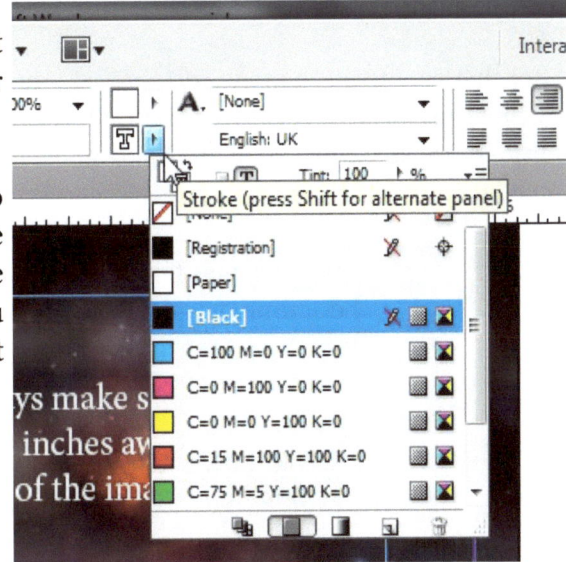

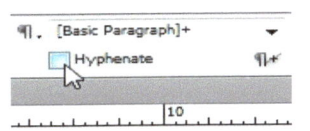

Repeat the process until you have finished adding your text.

Next, it's time to add page numbers. Use the text tool to draw text boxes in the outside, bottom corners of the page, but make certain you stay within the margin lines.

Then, go to *Type—insert special character—marker—current page number.*

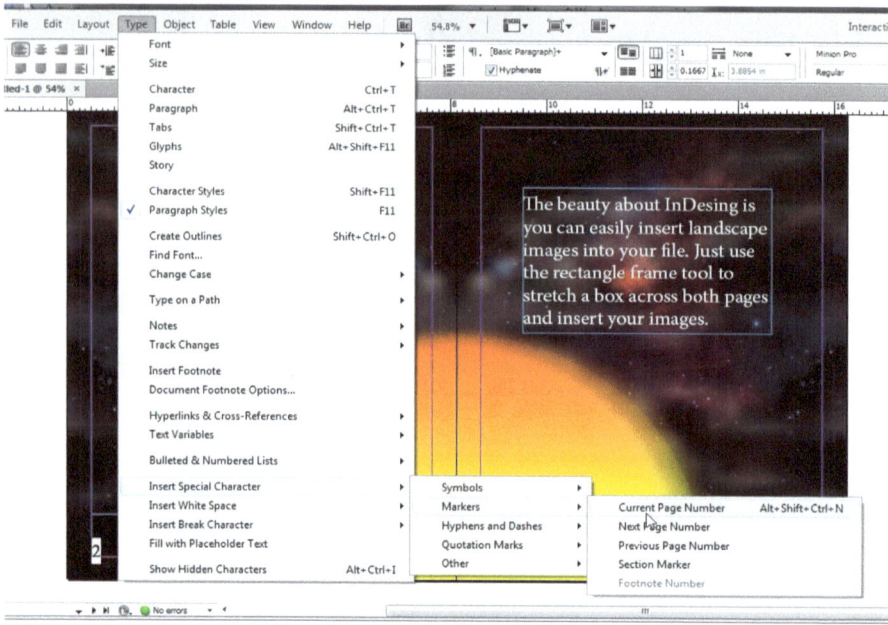

After that, you need to make certain that your page numbers begin with the first full image page as being page in. (Keep in mind that all odd page numbers must be on the right hand page and all even page numbers must be on the left hand page.)

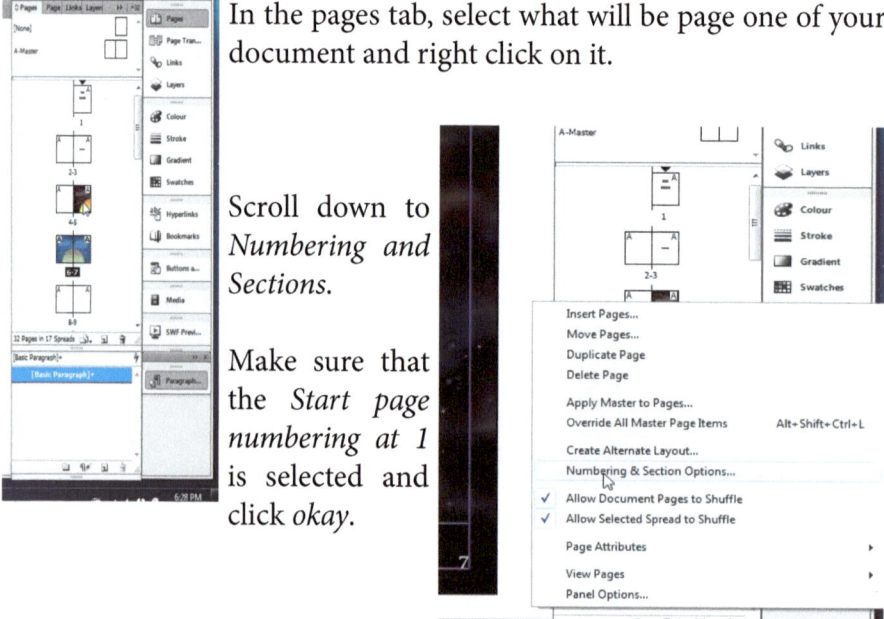

In the pages tab, select what will be page one of your document and right click on it.

Scroll down to *Numbering and Sections.*

Make sure that the *Start page numbering at 1* is selected and click *okay.*

You should get an upside down trian-
gle above the beginning of your new
section.

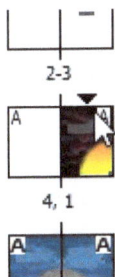

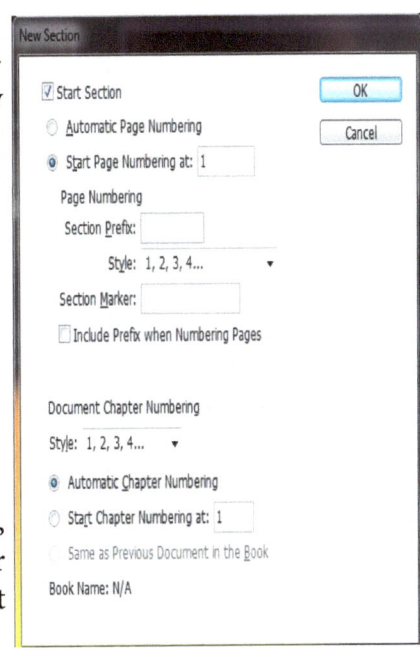

After you have inserted your images,
inserted your text, and put in your
page numbers, save the file one last
time.

Now, you need to export it, but before you do, go to *View—Display* and
make sure that *High Quality Print* is checked.

Then go to *File—Export*. A dialog box will show up.

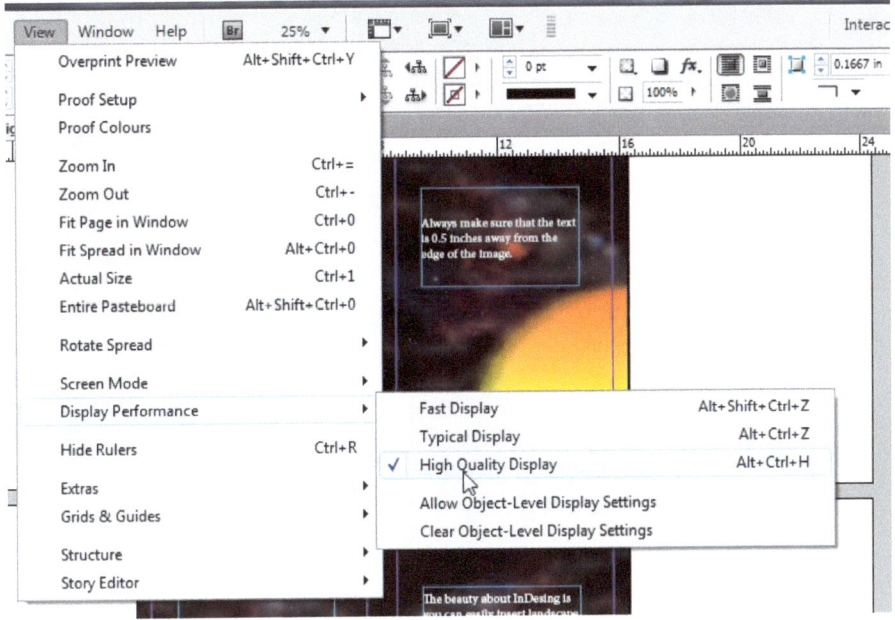

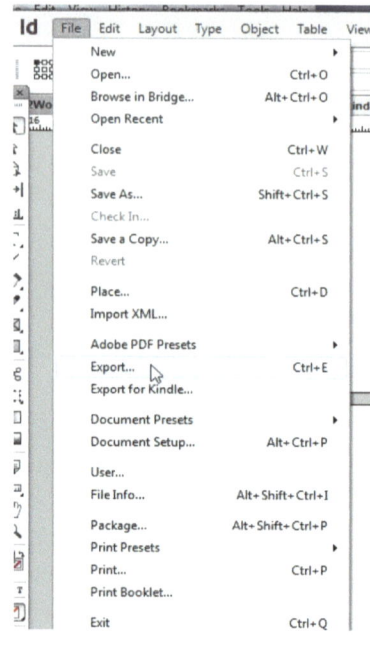

Type in the name of the file and choose the folder you want it saved in, Make sure that Adobe PDF is selected in the file type and hit *Save*. Next something like this should show up:

You want to make certain that *High Quality Print*, *all pages in range* and *Pages* is selected. Click *Export*. It can take anywhere from 5-10 minutes for InDesign to finish saving your files as a pdf. Once you have your pdf file, it is time for you to log in to your Createspace account and upload it.

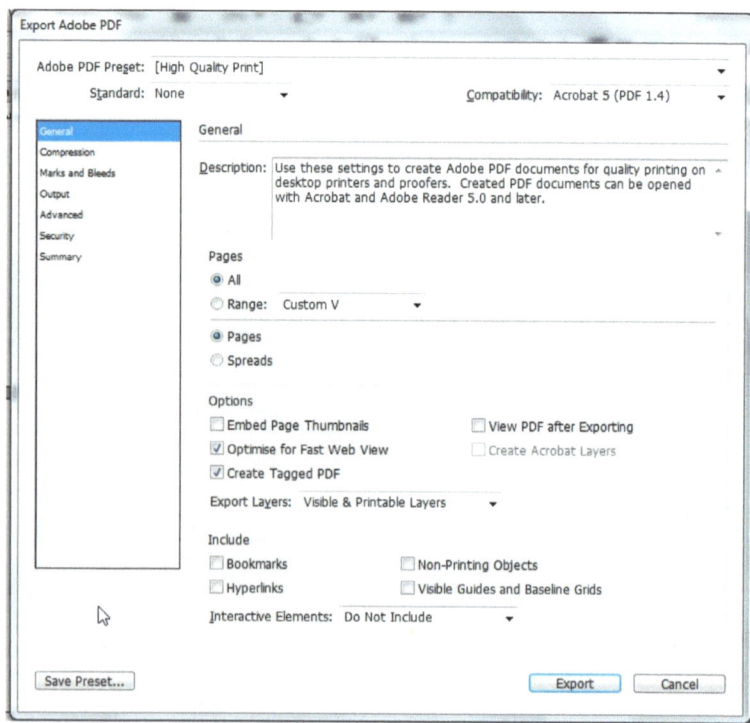

Without Full Bleeds Microsoft Word

Open Microsoft Word. Set up the three sections as explained in the Full Bleeds Formatting in Microsoft Word section above, except that instead of adding the 0.125" to your width and the 0.25" to your height, you will use the exact height and width of your chosen trim size for the page size. Basically, is you are doing an 8x10 book, then your pages size will be 8x10.

Go the margins dialog box. Type in the margins according to the Createspace margin chart above using a gutter of 0.375". Go to the paper tab. Click on custom size and type in your trim size. For instance, for an 8x10 trim size you will make the paper width 8 and height 10.

Put in your title page, copyright page, and dedication page. Go to section 2 of your document. insert your image(s). Because you are keeping the images within the margins, you can let word just size it for you. **Remember to save constantly.**

After you have inserted your images, save it one last time.

Close you file.

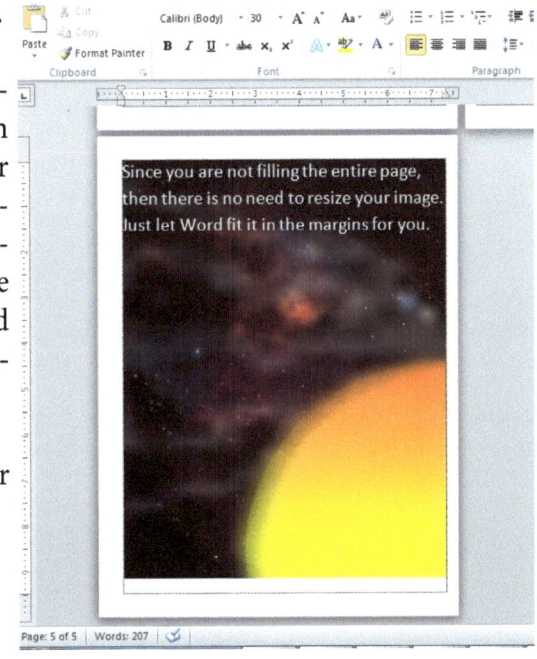

Open Adobe PDF and click on Create New PDF, or use one of the other options mentioned in the Full Bleed Microsoft Word Section). Select your book file. Once it has been converted make sure it looks the way you want it to. Save and close the file.

Yes, you can use Word's save as pdf function, but I don't recommend it as it is not reliable or consistent. However, if you wish to use it, go ahead.

Without Full Bleeds in InDesign

Set up your file as explained in the Full Bleeds in InDesign section, except make certain the page size is set to the exact size of your chosen book size. For instance, if you are making an 8x10 book, then the page size will be 8x10.

The margins will be 0.25 on all sides (I recommend using 0.5) with a gutter margin of 0.375.

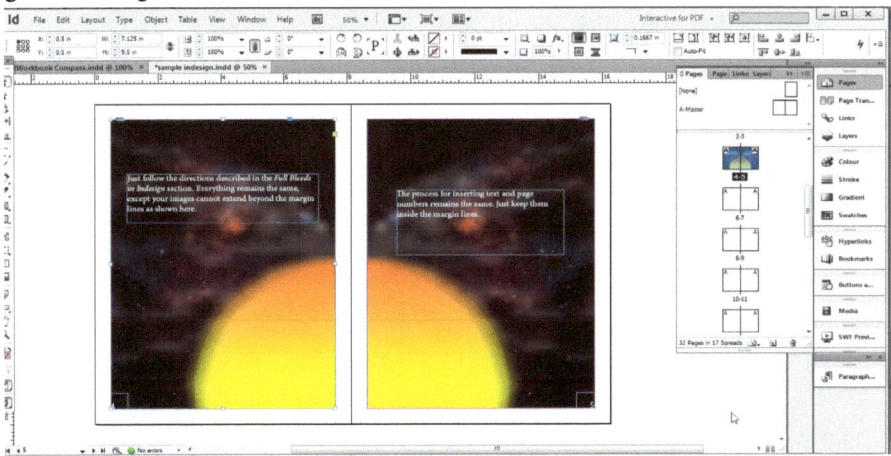

Follow the directions in the Full Bleeds Formatting in InDesign section on how to insert images, text, and page numbers, being certain to keep everything within the margins.

Once you have put in your images, text, and page numbers, save it and export your file as a PDF. Choose *High Quality Print*, *all pages in range*, and *Pages*. You DO NOT want to export the spreads.

And you're done!

How to Create a Book Cover

Creating a book cover for Createspace is very easy. You begin by calculating your spine width and cover dimensions.

Createspace's spine width chart is as follows:

For Black and White interior books.

> White Paper: multiply count by 0.002252

> Cream Paper: multiply count by 0.0025

For Color Interior books:

> Multiply page count by 0.002347

You calculate the spine width of you book with this equation: *number of pages x spine width calculation = spine width*

So let's say that you are doing a book that is 8.5 x 11 with 450 pages black and white on white paper.

400 x 0.002252 = 1.0134, or 1.01 (You usually only need the first 2 numbers to the right of the decimal point.)

1.01 is the spine width of your book.

To figure out the rest of the dimensions of your book, use the equation: width + spine width+ width = book dimension.

So, for a 450 page 8.5 x 11 size book with a black and white interior, the equation should look like:

8.5+1.01+8.5 = 19.01.

You don't need to calculate the height of the cover as the spine width does not affect it.

Open Photoshop (or Gimp if you're using that). Click on new project. For the width, use the total width that you just calculated your cover to be. Then, put in your height and make sure your dpi is set at 300.

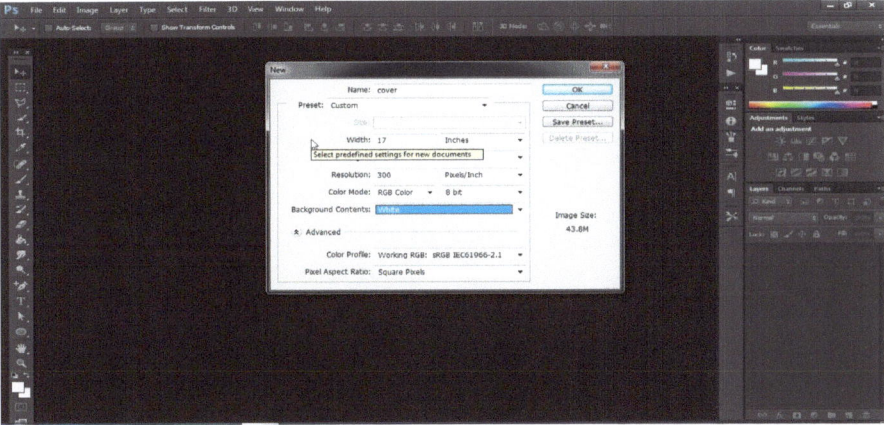

You should get a blank rectangular canvas. Before you do anything else, you need to put in your guidelines to section off the back cover, spine, front cover, and bleed areas. Click on *View—New Guide.*

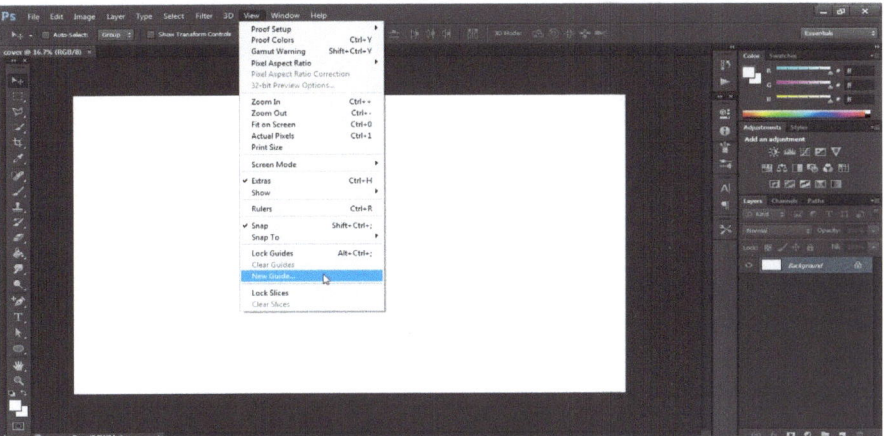

A. Olson

You will need to set up your horizontal and vertical guides. The first ones are easy as they should be set at 0.5.

The guides will go like this:

Horizontal guides setting off:

Bleed areas and spine

Marking off back cover:
- 0.5
- 8.5

Spine:
- 8.5625
- 9.4475

Marking off front cover:
- 9.51
- 17.51

Safe zones (where you probably don't want your text in):
- 8.25
- 9.76

You will get something that looks like this.

This will ensure that you don't put any text within the bleed area, or in an area where it could get distorted.

The image below is the same as the one above, except the bleed areas have been highlighted in blue, and the sections I like to call the safe zone are in yellow.

These guides set up your bleed areas, which are marked in blue in the images below.

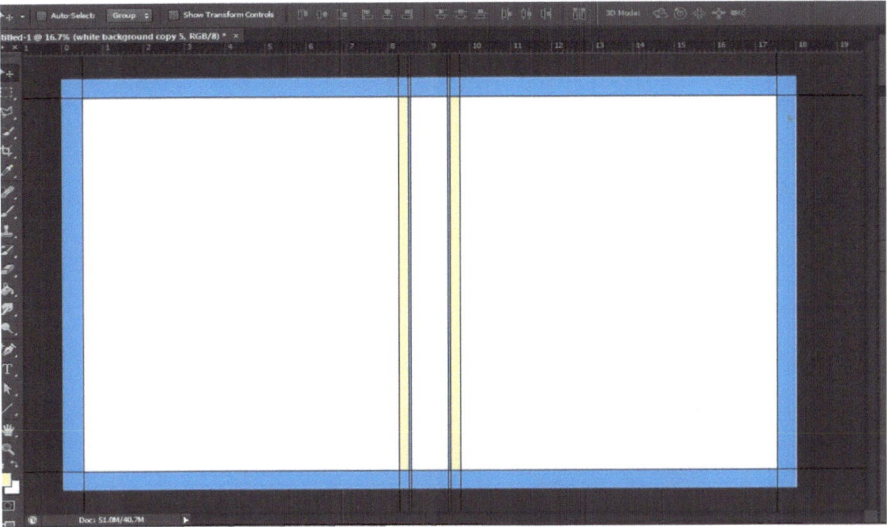

Next, insert the images you want to use for your front and back cover. You will go to new layer icon and click that. Then, go to *File—Place* and choose your image

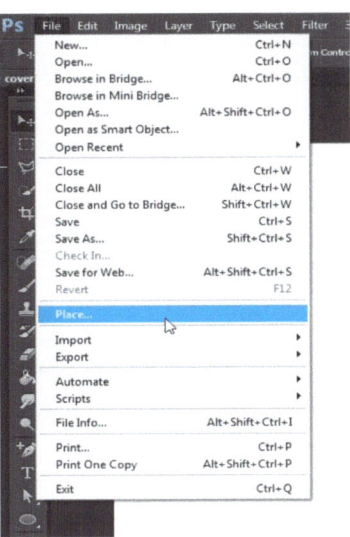

Repeat this process until all of your images are in and sized the way you want it.

If you can't see the guides, then change their color. Go to *Edit—Preferences— Guides, Grids, and Slices.*

And a dialog box will pop up. Choose the color you want your guides to be so that it shows up against your background images.

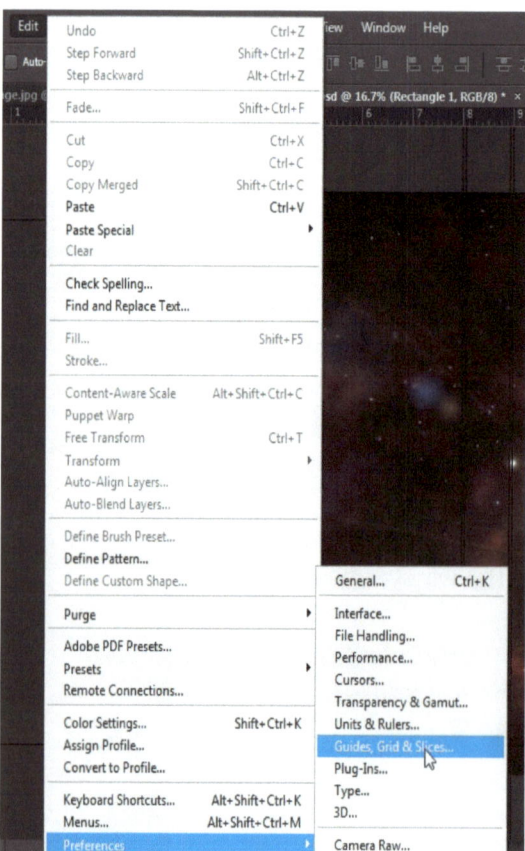

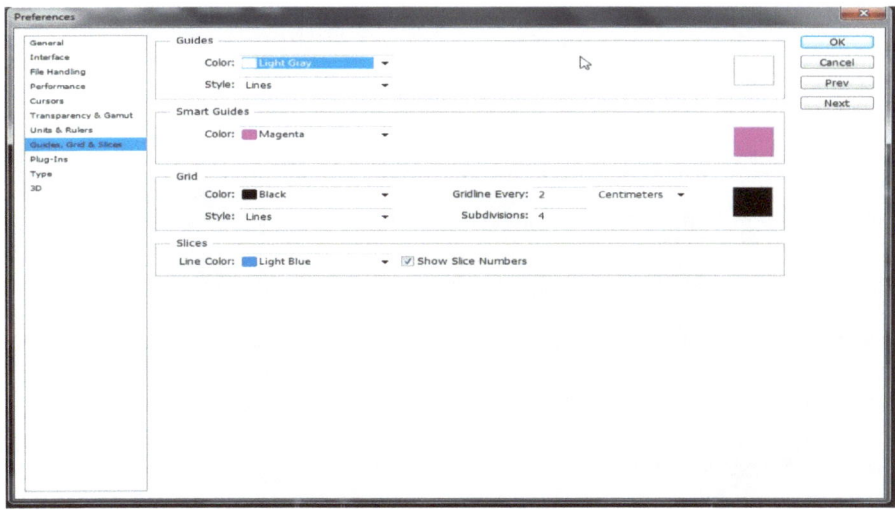

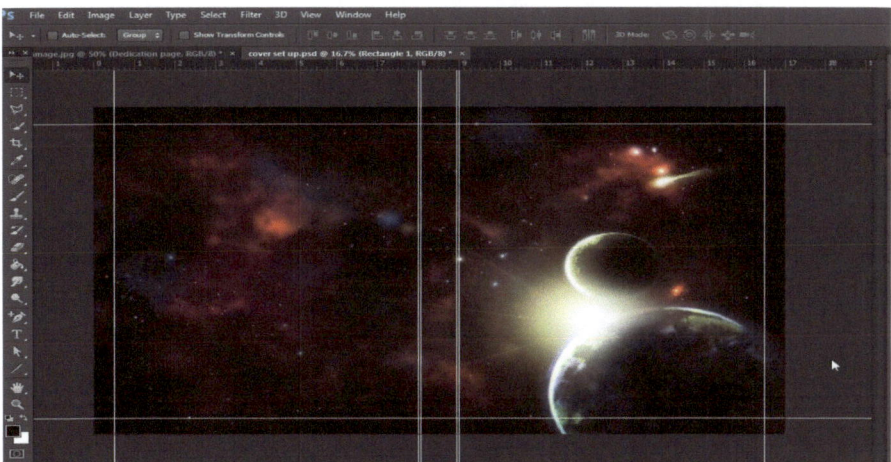

Choose the guides color and select *Okay.*

Once your images are in, add your text. Choose the text tool and draw a text box. Type in the title of the book. Choose your font color, font type and size, and test alignment.

Put the title and author name on the right hand side of the cover. Make sure you choose a crisp and clear font that is easy to read. I like to make the title of my books huge so people can see them from a distance, but the length of your title will determine the size of the font used. Just play with it until you get something you like.

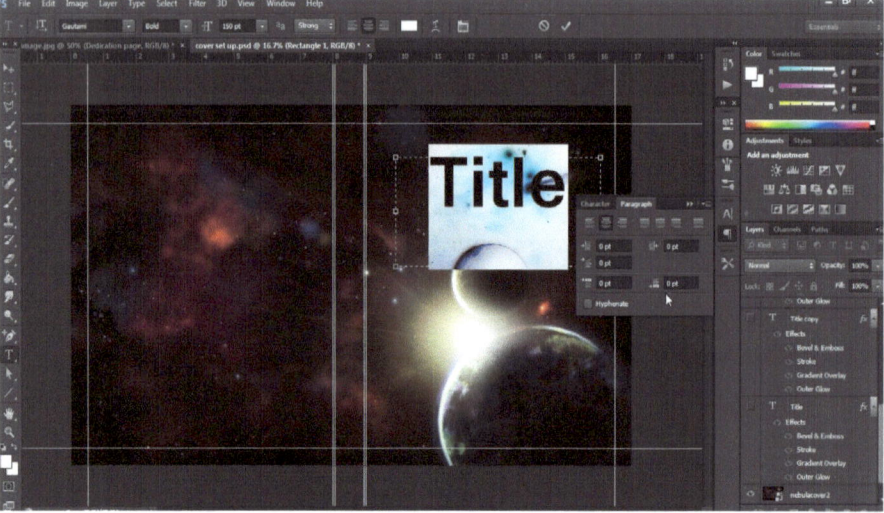

Next, you can add some text effects to make it stand out. Click the *fx* icon on the bottom right of your screen.

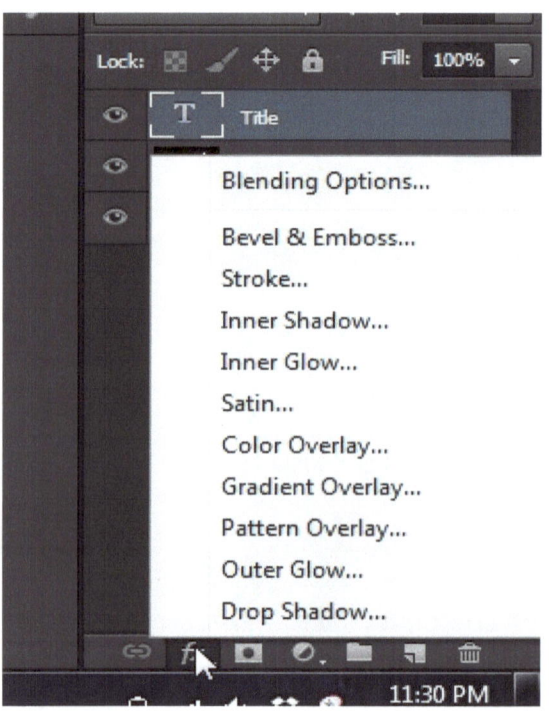

I chose to add a gradient and a stroke as show in the image below.

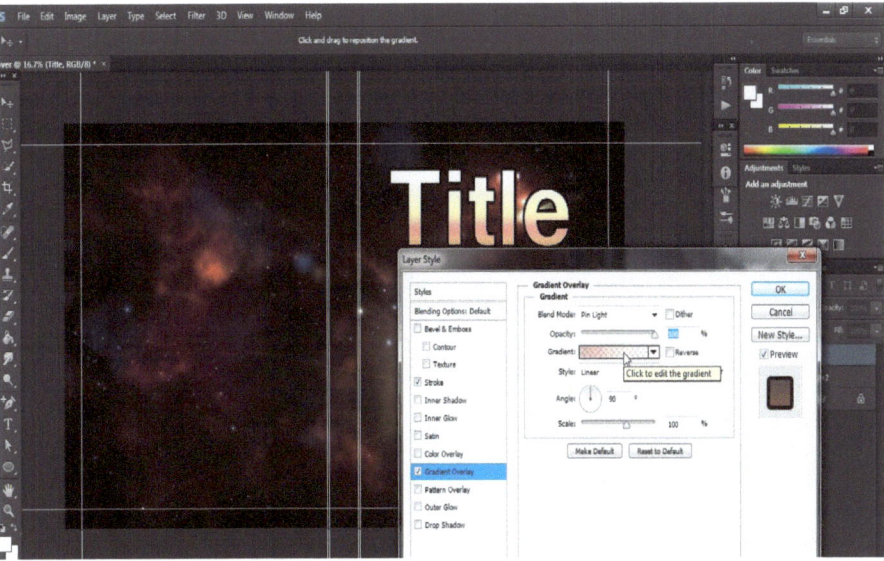

Then I added a *Bevel Emboss*. Just play with it until you get a result you want. I usually prefer the inner bevel with a depth of 100 or more.

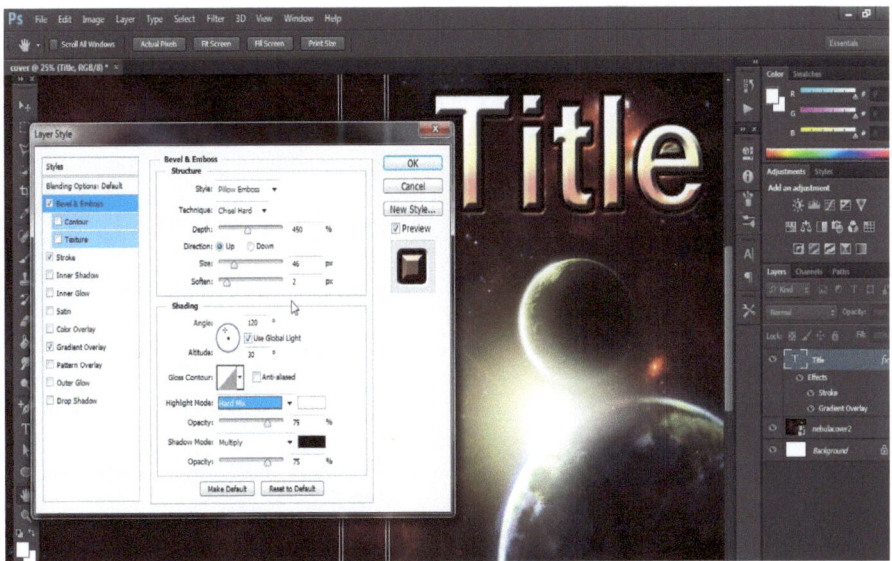

After that, I added a drop shadow. Choose your color and play with the angle and distance until you get the effect you want.

After that, I kept the same font style for the author name. This is usually

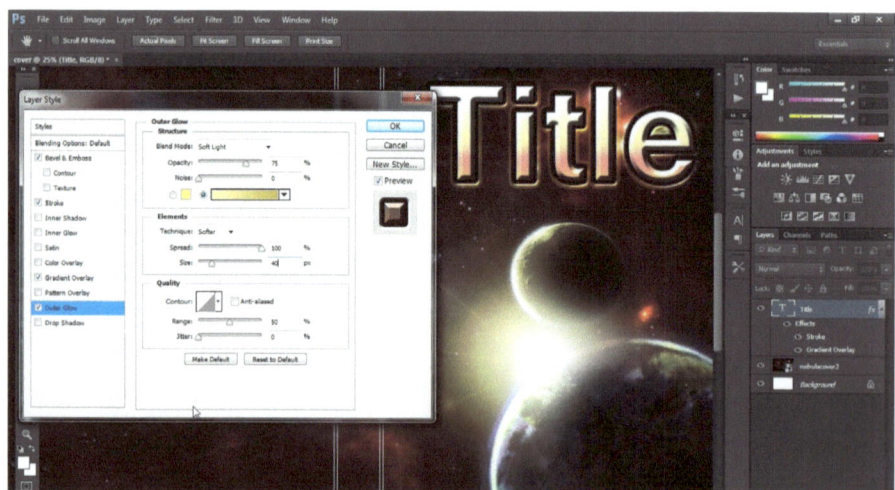

recommended. I clicked *crl—alt—j* to copy the title layer and clicked *okay*. Then, use the select tool to move the new layer down.

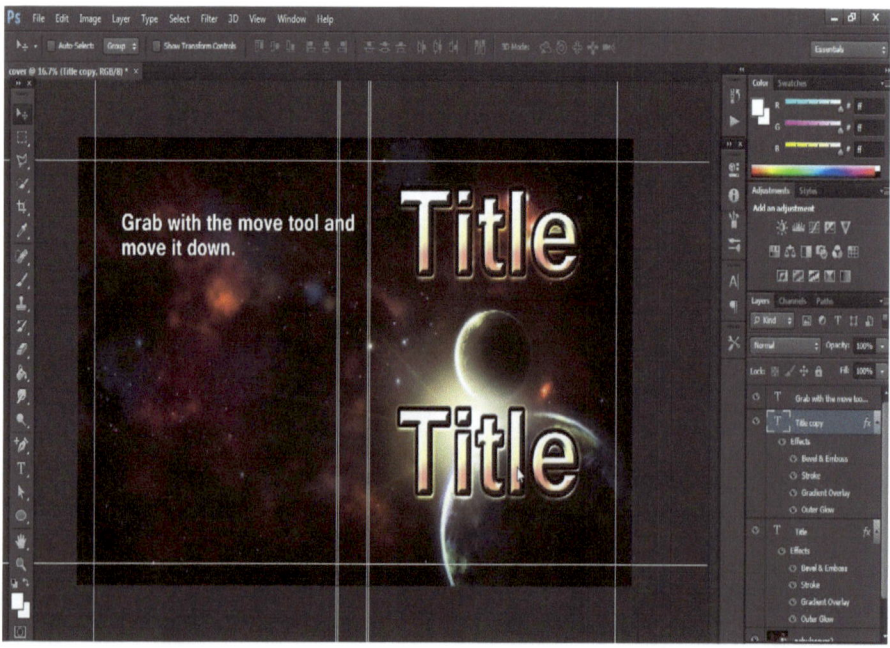

Select you type tool and click on the new title text. This should highlight it, allowing you to change it. Where you position the text on the cover, is up to you. I usually prefer to have the title at the top and the author name at the bottom.

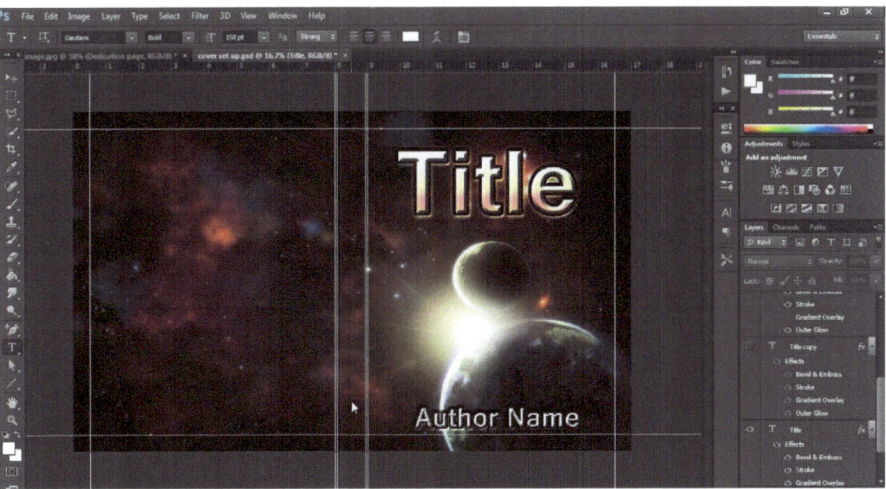

Next you want to put your title and author name text on the spine of your cover.

Note: If your book is 150 pages or less, it may not support spine text, in which case, you will have to leave it blank.

Select you author layer and click *ctrl—alt—j* to copy it. Select the copied layer and click *ctrl—T* to free transform it. Right click it and select *Rotate 90 CW.*

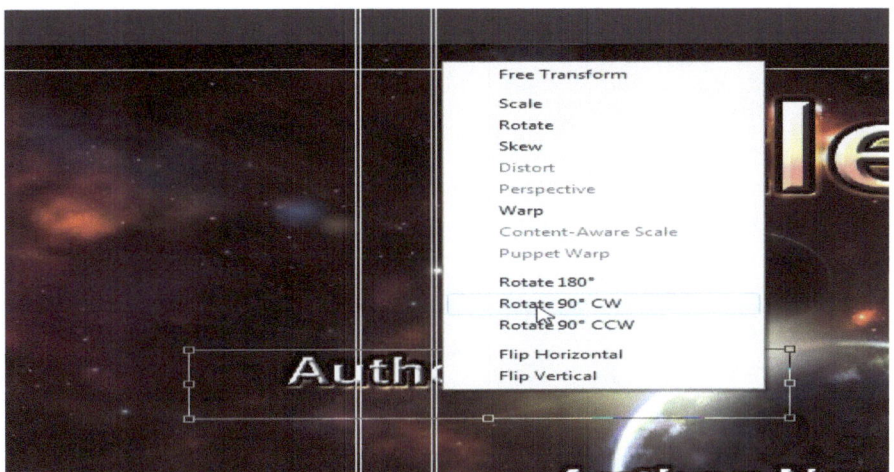

Position it on the spine and resize it so that it fits within the bleed lines. You may have to adjust the stroke and drop shadow effect so that it doesn't look overwhelmed by it, or stick out beyond the bleed line.

Once your front cover and spine text is positioned, you need to add your back cover content. Select the text tool again and draw another text box. Choose your font type, color, and font size. I recommend using somewhere between 11-14 size. Whether you add a stroke or not to outline it is up to you. Just make sure it is readable.

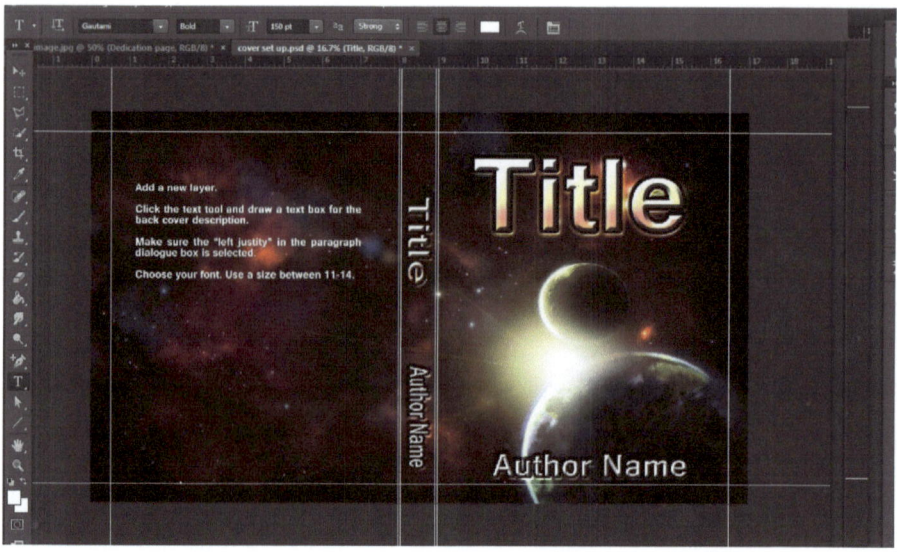

Next, you need to add a white box for your bar-
code. Click on the rectangle tool.

Make sure that Shape is selected and the fill col-
or is white with no stroke.

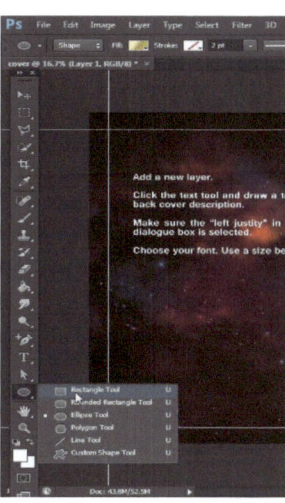

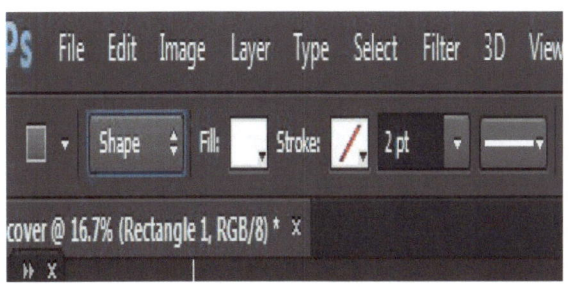

Draw the rectangle making it about 2 inches in width and 1 inch in
height. I usually place it on the bottom right of the back cover, within
the bleed lines. You can put it more in the center, if you wish.

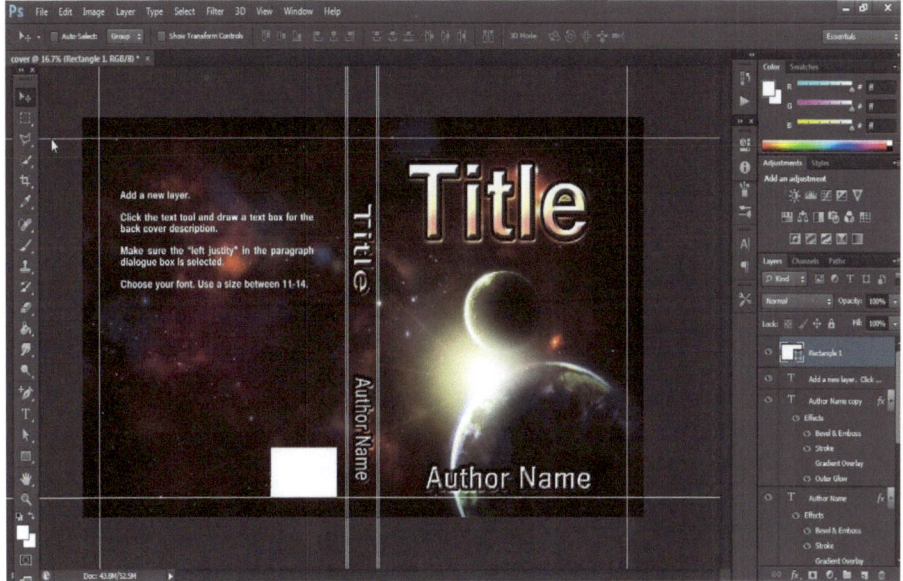

Once you have finished your cover, you need to save it as a JPEG image.
Go to *File—Save As*. Choose where you want to save the file, type in
the file name, and make sure that in the format box the JPEG option is
selected.

You can select PDF for the format if you want, since you will have to have it as a PDF file anyway, but I haven't had much luck with this.

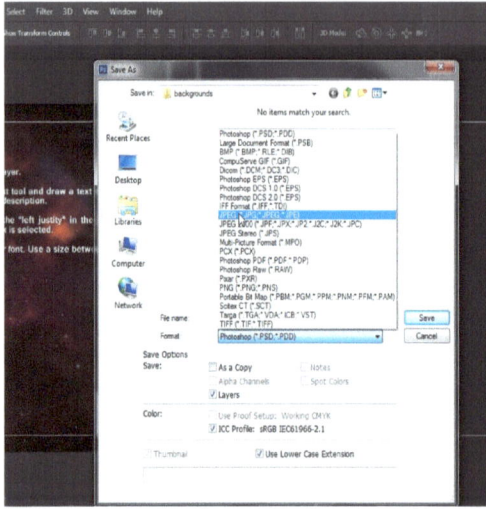

Click Save. A new box will pop up. Make certain that the image options is set to Maximum.

Open Adobe Acrobat and click on *Create New PDF*. Select your cover file. It will convert it and it should be the right size. Save it and close. Make sure that the file is less than 7 MB. Save it as a reduced sized pdf if necessary.

Now you are ready to upload it on Createspace.

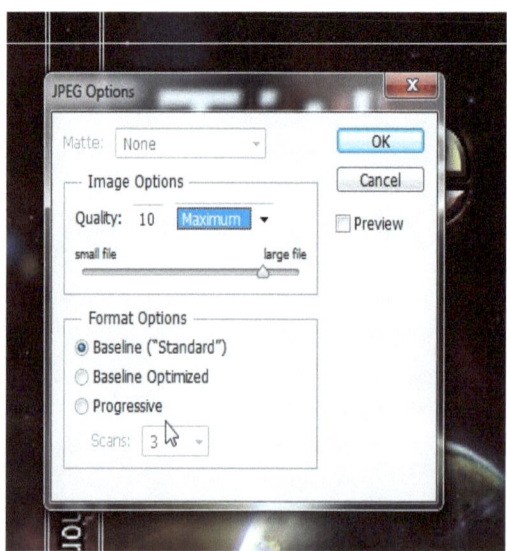

Upload to Createspace

Login to Createspace and add a new title. Enter all of your information. Make certain that the title and author's name you type in **match** what is in your interior and cover files **exactly**, otherwise it will be rejected in the review process.

Upload your interior file. Select *extends beyond page* for full bleeds; *ends before page* for inside bleeds. Go through the interior viewer. Make changes if you want, otherwise just save and continue.

In the cover section, upload your cover file by selecting *Upload a Cover Ready PDF*. Once everything has been filled in and uploaded, submit your files for review.

That's it! You're done! You have just created a full-color picture book all by yourself.

Kindle Formatting

Formatting your children's book for kindle is easy. First you need to create a KDP account if you do not have one already.

The best way to format your picture book for kindle is to use Kindle Comic Creator, which you can [download here](http://www.amazon.com/gp/feature.html?docId=1001103761) (http://www.amazon.com/gp/feature.html?docId=1001103761).

It's a free program, offered by Amazon that ensures your full page images will fill the entire kindle screen when formatted to mobi.

Before you create your kindle document, open your cover in Photoshop.

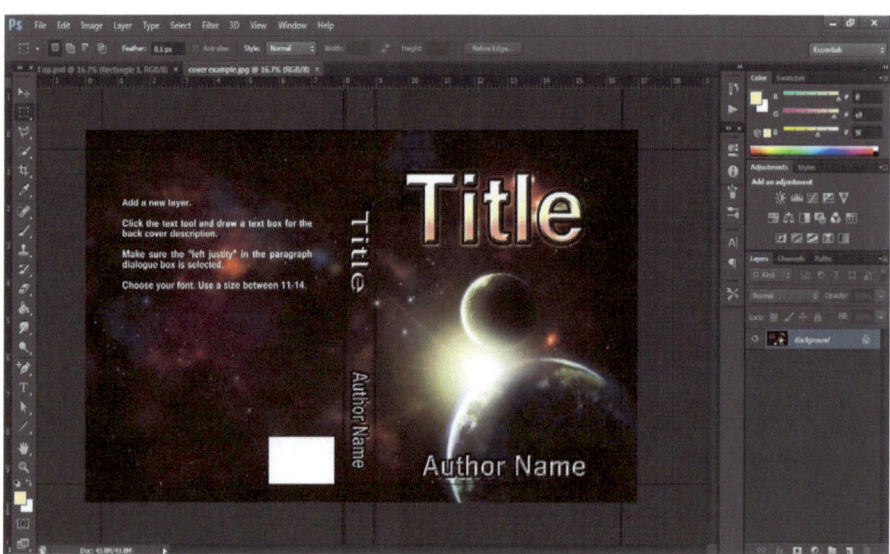

Click the crop tool on the left side of the screen.

And drag the box that shows up around your image until you have cropped out the front cover only.

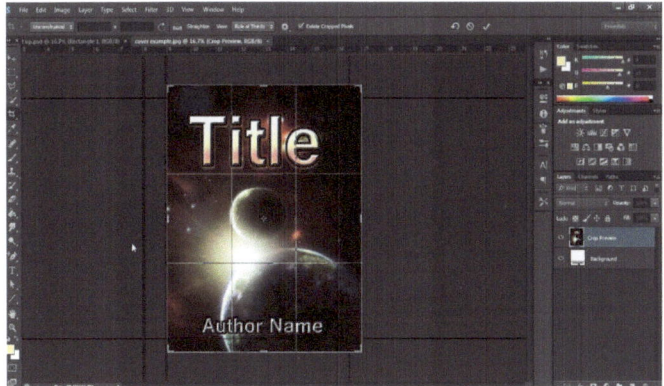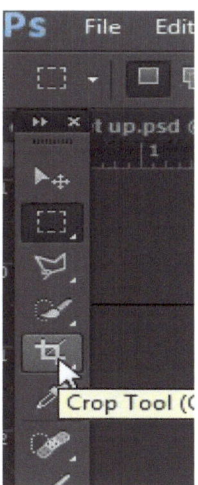

And hit enter.

Next, you need to resize the image to fit Amazon's specifications: of 9 inches in width and 13.5 inches in height and a resolution of 300 dpi.

Click *ctrl—alt—I*. You should get a dialog box like the image below.

Type in the appropriate width, height, and resolution to fit Amazon's specifications as mentioned above. Click *Okay*.

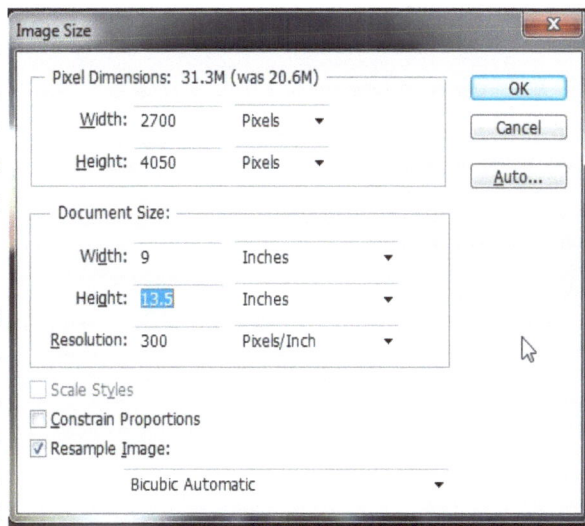

Next, click *ctrl—shift—S* and the save as dialog box should pop up. Make sure you give it a different file name and click *save*.. Then, click *Okay*.

Next you need to resize each of your images for kindle.

For portrait orientation:
- 800 pixels wide
- 1280 pixels height
- 96 dpi

For landscape orientation:
- 1280 pixels in width
- 800 pixels high
- 96 dpi

If you had embedded your text within your images already, before you started formatting it for Createspace, then just open your images and resize them.

If you used InDesign to format you Createspace book and the text was not embedded within the images, there are 2 ways to get your images with the embedded text:

1. Open you PDF file in Adobe Acrobat Standard, click on *Save As—Image—JPEG*. And make sure you save everything in a separate folder. This will take all of your PDF pages and convert them to JPEGs.

2. Open each image in Photoshop, resize it to 800 x 1280 pixels (for portrait) or 1280 x 800 pixels (for landscape) add the text to it following the instructions from Formatting Your Images.

Make sure you save your images with different names, such as Kindle-image1, and so forth. Also, create a new folder on your desktop to your newly formatted kindle images in. This will make it easier for you to find them later. Once you have sized and saved your images, close Photoshop and open Kindle Comic Creator and select *Create New Book*.

Then follow their wizard. Choose your language,

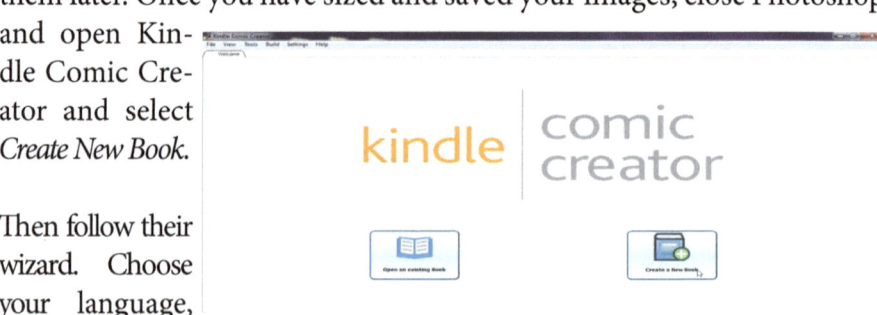

whether your book is portrait or landscape, left to right scrolling, and type in your image size.

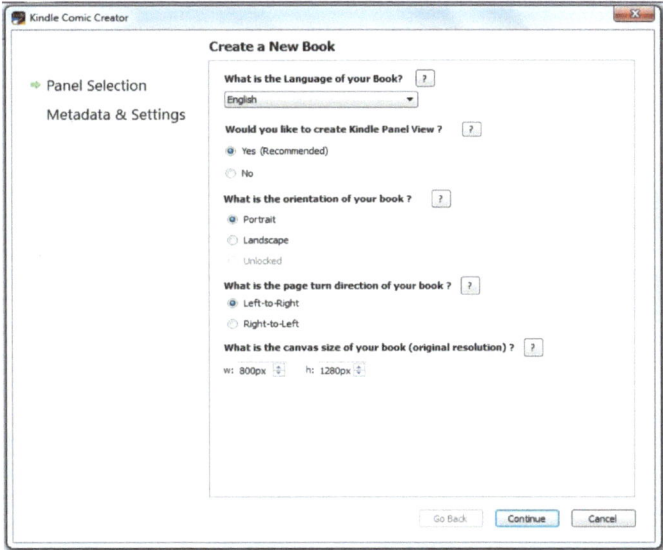

Click *Continue.*

Then, you will put in the title, author name, and publisher data. In the cover image section, click the browse button and locate your cover. Then, choose where you want your built mobi file to be saved. Click *Start Adding Pages.*

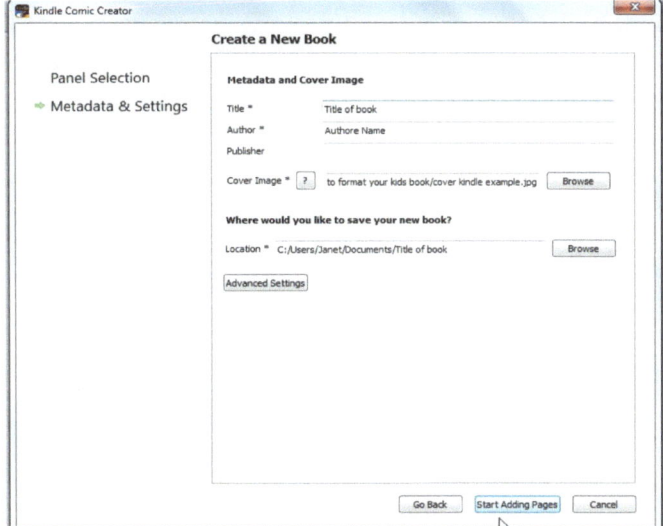

This will take you to a dialog box where you locate your kindle image files, select them all, and click *Okay*. Your images will have been inserted.

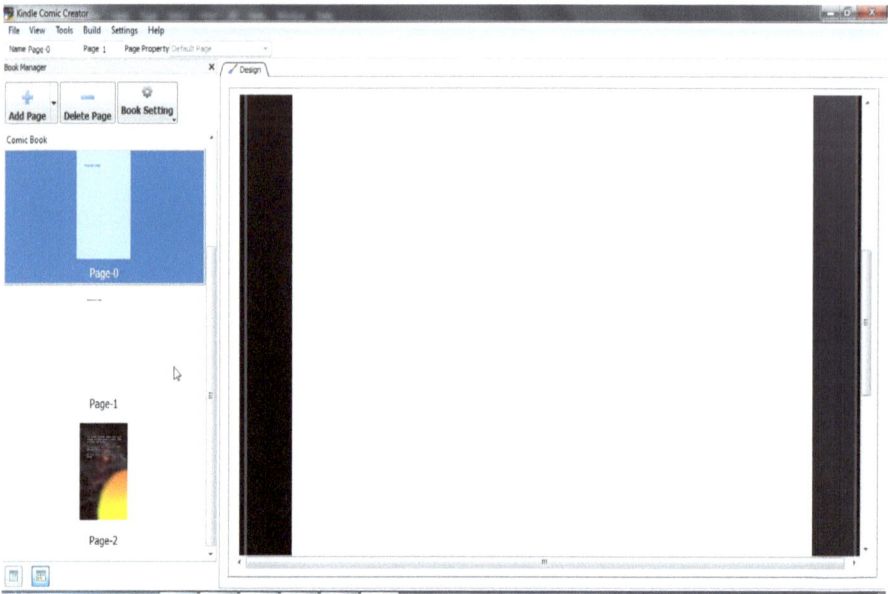

You can add pages, delete pages, and move pages around. Make sure you save your working file. Sometimes, Kindle Comic Creator freezes, depending on how many images you have. When you are ready to build your file, go to *Build—Build and Preview*.

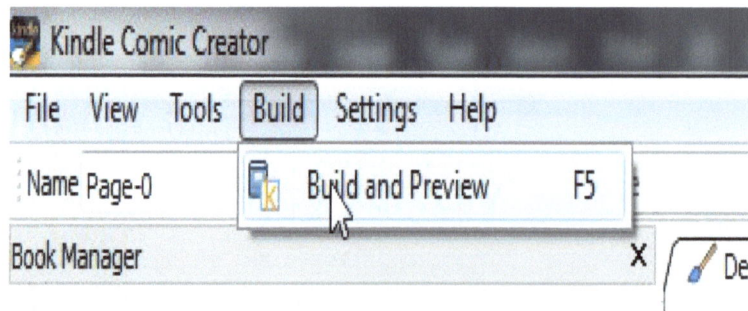

The program will run and build your file. Once the mobi file has been created, you should get something that looks like this, giving you a preview of your kindle book.:

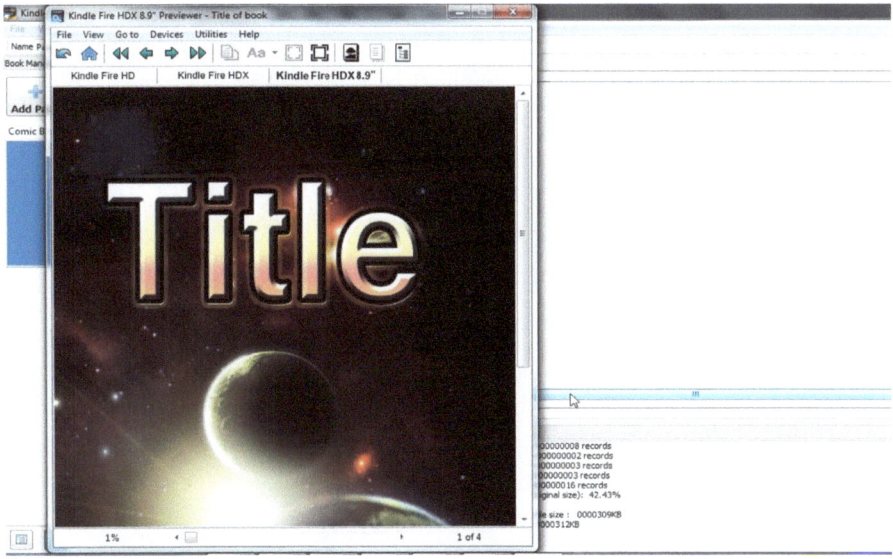

Scroll through it and make sure it is as you want it.

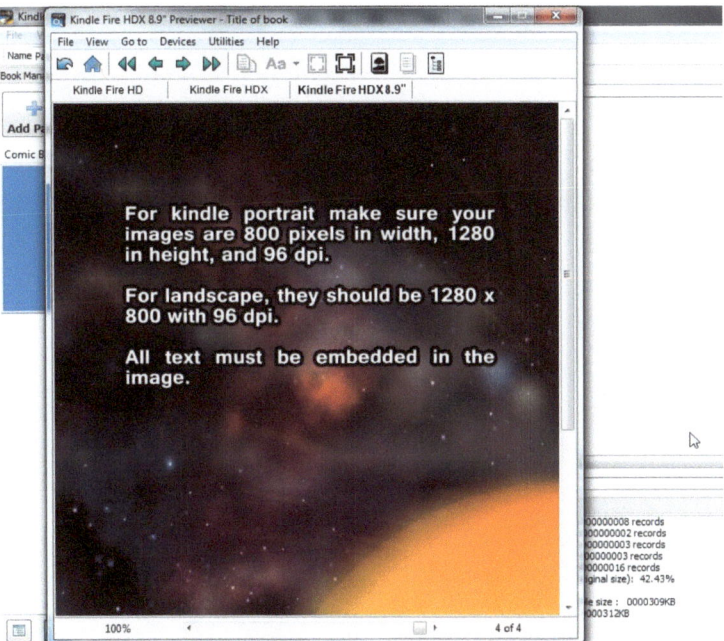

Once done, close the program.

To upload to KDP, login to your account and click on Add New Title.

Fill in the required information. When you reach the area for uploading your book file, look up the mobi file you created and upload it.

Make sure you preview your book before going to the next section. The images should fill the page. After you have uploaded your book, set up your pricing and royalties, and submit for publication.

Afterthoughts…

I hope this book has been helpful for you. If it has, or hasn't, please leave a review and share your thoughts. If you have other helpful hints about publishing picture books, leave that as well. Feedback is always welcome.

Good luck with your writing and I wish you success in your publishing career.

From the Author

I hope you found this ebook helpful and that it saved your hours of frustration on formatting your children's book for Createspace.

To let others know about the value of this book, share your thoughts and story on publishing on Createspace. It allows other readers to decide if they wish to purchase the book, but it also allows me, as the author, to know where improvements can be made for updated versions. Once again, thank you for reading this book and I hope it proves useful.

Leave your review here (http://www.amazon.com/Format-Your-PiICTURE-Book-Createspace-ebook/dp/B00C1QKBOQ/ref=s-r_1_1?ie=UTF8&qid=1430268756&sr=8-1&keywords=format+-for+createspace):

way to format children's books.

Open your image editing software. I use Photoshop. I made the decision to ditch the free software and just purchase the CS6 version and have not regretted it. Click on file—new project and set up your image size, bleeds, and margins. For instance if you are creating an 8x10 book then you will need to create and 8.125" x 10.25" image. This is because Createspace requires that your images extend beyond the page margin: 0.125" for width and 0.25" for height. The formula goes like this:

Width trim size + 0.125 = total width

Height trim size + 0.25 = total height

So for an 8x10 book your images and interior pages must be formatted to 8.125 x 10.25 in dimension.

For a 5x7 book with full bleeds, pages in the interior file must be 5.125 x 7.25.

This is why I format images to the full page dimensions so that when I create the interior file, the images do not look blurry. And if you want to play it safe, make your images larger than the page size. For instance, if you are making an 8x10 book, you can make your images 9x11. Once your new project is created, you will have a blank canvas.

www.ingramcontent.com/pod-product-compliance
Lightning Source LLC
Chambersburg PA
CBHW050820290526
45792CB00001B/195